Rapid Reading

Kathryn Redway has worked in industry in Europe, the UK and the USA. She has managed her own company for the past five years. The company specialises in various facets of management and educational training and has clients in industry and the educational and public services.

Kathryn is French but lives in England. She travels extensively, lecturing and consulting. Her special interests include self-development studies, innovation in industry and the public services, travel, food and wine.

Kathryn M. Redway
Rapid Reading

Pan Original
Pan Books London, Sydney and Auckland

First published 1988 by Pan Books Ltd,
Cavaye Place, London SW10 9PG
9 8 7 6 5 4 3 2 1
© Kathryn M. Redway 1988
ISBN 0 330 30417 8
Photoset by Rowland Phototypesetting Ltd, Bury St Edmunds, Suffolk
Printed and bound in Great Britain
by Richard Clay Ltd, Bungay, Suffolk

To
Peter and Michael Duncan

Acknowledgements

I wish to express my thanks to:

- Tony Buzan and Brian Helweg-Larsen, who introduced me to the subject and guided me in my early days with it

- Cristina Stuart, who suggested I write this book

- Alison Leach, whose friendship, encouragement and comments were invaluable when I started it

- Susan Mosely Harris, whose experience and comments were particularly helpful

- Norman Duncan for taking the time to sharpen my style and inspiring my enthusiasm in this and other areas

- Peter Bruggen for his unfailing support for my work

- All my students who taught me to listen and inspired much of the contents of this book

And, of course, Keith, my husband, whose patience, support and suggestions made me finish the book.

None of these people is responsible for any errors of fact or interpretation in this book.

The author and publishers also wish to thank the following publishers, authors and agents for permission to reprint copyright material:

Agenzia Letteraria Internazionale for an extract from *The Europeans* by Luigi Barzini; *The Economist* for the article 'Deutsche Bank makes its mark' from 25 July 1987 issue; *The Times Newspapers Ltd* for the article 'Pohl walks tightrope of German concensus' from 25 June 1987 issue; James Edmonds for his article 'Timesharing – the Club/Trustee System' and A. K. Redway for his article 'Management Tools – Project Planning Procedures'

Contents

Introduction

Why buy and read this book?

YOU .... have picked up . . .

THIS BOOK .... to flick through it, to see if it is
worth reading or buying.

RAPID READING .... is . . .

SIMILAR .... to the actions you carry out to determine
if you want . . .

TO BUY .... or read this book now.

GLANCE .... at and understand the . . .

TITLE, ... cover illustration, the . . .

TABLE OF CONTENTS

. . . and chapter headings. Flick through the book to see illustrations and layout, and read through one or two paragraphs. The approach to reading and memorising described in this book is similar to the process you have just completed. By looking down the left-hand column above you have skimmed the . . .

KEYWORDS .... to assess the value of the book to you.
You have done your . . .

FIRST RAPID READ.

The *purpose* of this book is to enable professional people and others such as students, to *assimilate quickly* and *use* documents such as *magazines* and *textbooks* more *effectively*. Many of us have a lot of literature – papers and professional or official documents – to deal with and *information* to absorb and recall. By learning to read rapidly you can *increase* (typically tenfold) your *effectiveness* in dealing with documents and the information they contain.

The aim of this book is to boost your confidence and build
on what you already know. It gives you a flexible technique
which you can adapt to YOUR needs.

This book is based on the attitudes and comments of many
businessmen and students who have attended the author's
courses. The questions they have raised; the difficulties, as well
as the enthusiasm, have been recorded. This book should often
mirror your own thoughts and respond to them.

How to use this book

Rapid reading is not just reading faster, but is also the technique
of focusing on what you need. The approach of this book is to
emphasise the importance of **setting objectives before** you start
reading. Identify now what you need most and go to the sections
of the book which supply your needs. You do not have to follow
this book – or any other textbook – sequentially from page one to
the end.

A key part of rapid reading lies in the selection of what you
need from a document. Things you already know, or which are of
no interest or use to you must be ignored. This means that rapid
reading consists of learning **where** to find information and **how to
interpret it**. Many documents contain information you do not
need now, but it is very useful to remember where it is, so that
you may refer to it later if you need it.

Use this book in the same manner that you use any other
document:

■ do you want to find out what it contains?
■ do you want to summarise the contents?
■ do you want to learn a part of the contents?

If, after your first search through the book you decide that you
need more, go back; but only after you have completed your
initial rapid read.

Also, remember that if you enjoy what you are doing, it will be
much more effective.

Who should read this book?

The average professional person with 1.8 children reads four fiction novels and two professional textbooks per year and each month reads thoroughly one professional magazine and skims (ineffectively) through two other journals connected with their work. All this reading occupies, perhaps, one hundred hours per year. This book enables you to either cut this reading time to ten hours per year, with more effective selection of information, retention and recall, or read about ten times as much in the same amount of time.

This book is also for people who read few books, because they are discouraged even before they start. To them, many books appear long and, if they are not well presented, intimidate the reader. Many of these readers start on page 1 and laboriously plod through page after page, taking a long time, whilst others will give up early and set a pattern of never reading or finishing a book. For all readers there is a better and quicker way to go about the process.

The difference between readers: professional people and students

Many adult professional people and students use the same reading methods, but they are dissatisfied with the results. The dissatisfaction stems from the fact that they are still using the method which they learned **as children**. They do not appreciate that their purpose in reading is totally different from their reading requirements when they were young and that they should, therefore, be using different reading techniques from those they learned originally.

Some school students, and even undergraduates, are required to learn some subjects, (for example, economics, law, biology or accounting) practically by heart. Missing just one word in a test may give the student poor marks. Consequently, these students read with the sole purpose of learning by rote; often they do not comprehend what they are learning.

A professional, on the other hand, reads because he is interested in a report; or material piles up in his in-tray; or because he has to prepare quickly for a meeting, and his boss has just dumped something on his desk. Whatever the reason, no one is going to ask him, word for word, what he has read. Thus, his reading method and degree of comprehension should be more flexible.

1 What is reading?

In this chapter . . .

Rapid reading is a skill. Your success in mastering the skill depends on your attitude; your enthusiasm and readiness to try a technique. You must:

- Want to improve
- Be confident that you will do so

The myths surrounding the reading process are discussed and the reasons why you must abandon them are explained. The facts are that:

- Reading for both pleasure and work can be fast
- Regression is not necessary to aid comprehension
- Reading can be fun and variable
- Skimming can be reading
- Technical documents can be read rapidly
- You do not need to try to remember everything you read

This chapter describes how the brain is used as you read and how the proper use of both the left and right hemispheres of the brain facilitates rapid reading. By means of a simple exercise you can determine your initial reading speed and the extent of your comprehension. Then, after learning why comprehension is subjective and how bad habits – such as subvocalising and lack of concentration – can be changed, you will be taken (in following chapters) through a short sequence of exercises designed to increase your reading speed.

Reading is an attitude

This book will give you a systematic approach to improving your reading. But if you are not committed to improvement and do not have a strong belief in your ability to do so, the technique will not work. You must have two things:

- The wish to improve. This can only come from you. You wish to improve because you are a slow reader and you want to read more and because you MUST read, yet you find it difficult to be interested in the material
- A confident attitude. Knowing that you want to improve AND believing that you can, then you must simply trust yourself and the advice and information given in this book

Part of a positive mental attitude – the desire to improve – requires you to be optimistic. Accept that learning to read faster is a process of 'highs' and 'lows'. Each step contains an essential element that contributes to acquiring the technique. Do not look for difficulties **before** you start. Do not analyse each step **until** you have completed it.

First admit that you must change your habits if you want to read faster. You do not yet know how: that's what this book will tell you. Remember, suspend judgement until you have given the technique a fair trial.

Embarking on something new is an opportunity to extend your knowledge. It will be easier if you can relax and have fun as you go along. This skill makes the same demands upon the learner as acquiring any other new skill, say skiing. Be child-like in your attitude. Children quickly sense the exhilaration of other children who can already ski. Their sole objective is to be able to enjoy themselves in the same way. They learn quickly because that objective is always before them. They accept short-term setbacks, like falling over. Being child-like is being unafraid to make mistakes. That is learning: finding out what works and what does not work. They do not question the instructions. Today you are on the nursery slopes, with a limited speed. No-one will know of your mistakes as you learn to read. Look to the top of the mountain and be determined that you, too, will enjoy the thrill of speed.

Getting rid of myths

There are many myths surrounding the reading process. Here are a few we need to get rid of:

A good pleasure-read and thorough work reading has to be slow

There is no evidence to support this view at all. Slow readers, in fact, find pleasure-reading too time-consuming to be enjoyable. This, of course, makes such readers reluctant even to start. Slow reading discourages the reader because there are so few early rewards. Slow readers get a fragmented comprehension. They miss the overall driving idea and meaning of the material, in the same way as a copy-typist who necessarily reads every word may not take in what she types. Her mind wanders off because reading is at the pace of typing – slow and dull. But, fast reading, as explained in this book will prove pleasant for leisure reading and effective for work reading.

When you fail to comprehend or lose concentration, immediately re-read

This is one of the most common faults of poor readers – going back to check what you have just read – to try to gain understanding. It is very inefficient. It slows you down. It allows your mind to wander off. It sidetracks you from anticipating what is coming. It distracts you from thinking actively.

A simple technique for increasing comprehension and concentration is to maintain a dialogue with the author. Question the author: why did he say that? Is it different from what he said before? Anticipate what the author will say in the next section of the document.

Reading is boring

This myth is popular with those who believe in myths 1 and 2. Reading is fun and rewarding if you are motivated, follow a rhythm and actively seek information. Reading fast, understanding it and retaining what is read is even more exciting.

Skimming can't be reading

Skimming IS reading. It is THE technique to apply when you are looking for something specific and you want to overview a whole document. Skimming is taking mental note of the presentation of material, picking up what stands out and reading headings and keywords. It is a vital part of rapid reading, sometimes used by itself, but more often in conjunction with other steps. (See Chapters 3 and 4.)

You need long periods of time to read

You don't. If you know how to skim you can pick up ideas from any document, effectively, in five minutes. But efficient and rapid reading requires concentration. You need to concentrate as soon as you decide to read. When you know what your objectives are, reading can be done in five or fifteen minutes slots. Long periods spent reading are certainly not synonymous with efficient reading.

Technical documents can't be read rapidly

Such documents lend themselves very well to rapid reading. In most cases these documents give background information which the reader does not need, at least to begin with. Rapid reading is a series of steps. The key step, in the case of technical reports, is to decide beforehand what you are seeking. Then you skim for this material, skimming more carefully when you locate important passages. Of course, there will be more solid material in such documents than in a novel. The speed used to read the chosen material will be slower than for a novel. To master the skill of speed reading is to master flexibility – that is, use different speeds for different materials.

Rapid reading everything will be boring

Not so. Rapid reading involves a great variety of approaches which keep reading dynamic and challenging. You adjust your speed according to the material itself and your purpose in reading it.

When you read you need to remember everything

That might have been true at school, but not any more. Read the section of this book entitled 'The difference between readers: professional people and students' in the Introduction.

This myth is a symptom of insecurity. You know it is an impossible task and seek protection behind it. It allows you to say: 'I told you it was impossible. I can't do it.' If this is a myth that you subscribe to, stop, and evaluate your reading situation and requirements. You need to set achievable targets. Assess your familiarity with the subject; define your goals for this reading; and decide what you need to remember.

The brain and reading

When you pick up a book with the intention of reading all or parts of it, what happens? The eyes see the words on the pages. The words are made of letters, or symbols which you also recognise. The word evokes an image and a meaning: the word is understood. Next, the word is made part of a sentence. You connect the words and understand their meaning. You then relate the information in this sentence to other sentences and to the rest of your knowledge: this is comprehension. Depending on how often you use this information, you retain this comprehension for a short or long period.

In summary, when you read, you perform the following tasks:

- Visual recognition of the symbols
- Assimilation of the symbols into meaningful images reinforced by sounds or any of the other senses
- Integration into semantic – or related – comprehension
- Retention
- Prepare for recall

Thus, reading is a complex process and it involves different and distinctive steps and activities. It is difficult to pinpoint where reading takes place in the brain because, for each activity, you shuttle information between the two halves, or hemispheres, of the brain.

The brain consists of two hemispheres, the left and the right, which perform different functions. Each hemisphere specialises in certain types of activities (see Figure 1.1).

In right-handed people, the left hemisphere deals with numbers, language and analytical thought. It processes ideas sequen-

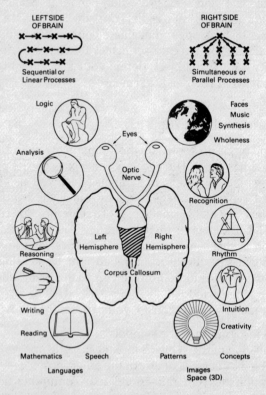

Figure 1.1 View from above or plan of the brain
Activities listed for most right-handed people

tially or works in a step-by-step or linear manner. The right hemisphere is better at handling concepts of wholeness, patterns, recognition, visual imagery, space, music and rhythm and processes ideas simultaneously or in parallel.

Many left-handed people have these brain processes reversed. Apparently over ninety per cent of right-handed people, but only about sixty per cent of left-handed people, deal with numbers, language and analysis in the left hemisphere of the brain (see A. Searleman, p. 93). We do not yet know why this difference exists.

The two hemispheres are connected by an intricate mass of nerve cells called the corpus callosum which works in rather the same way as a telephone exchange: it links the two sides and makes them communicate.

At first appearance, reading is linear; it seems to be a step-by-step approach since it deals with a sequence of words. This description would make it an activity which, for the majority of people, is done in the left hemisphere. But efficient reading is more than that: it requires the use of visual imagery: it demands that some 'whole' be seen, and that a pattern be anticipated. Also, reading is faster and easier if a rhythm is imposed as we move along. Reading involves using BOTH sides of our brain. Skilled readers shuttle information automatically and unconciously from left to right and vice-versa. Active reading forces the reader to connect ideas simultaneously and to think faster.

How do you read?

Let's find out. The passage that follows will assess the speed at which you read, the extent of your comprehension, and the habits that you have. Please observe the following instructions:

1 Have a stopwatch or a watch with a second hand ready.
2 Choose a comfortable place to read where you will not be interrupted.
3 Try to read as you would normally: don't speed up or slow down because it is an exercise.

4 Have a notebook by your side.
5 Note the time when you start and when you finish reading
  the passage.
6 Read the passage **once only**, from 'Quote' to 'Unquote'.

Quote.
The men who, at turning points of history, managed to make the
French behave as a great nation and sometimes led them to
victory, to grandeur, and to prosperity, are the immortal heroes
of French history. School children recite their names like those of
saints in litanies. Among them are (as François Maurras said) 'the
Forty Kings who made France': Clovis, the king of the Franks,
who gave the country its name and its religion, Hugh Capet, the
first king, Philippe Auguste, Saint Louis, Henry IV, Louis
XIV . . . Added to them, there are a young peasant girl, Jeanne
d'Arc, and one fanatical and meticulous organiser of bureaucracy
(he and his men worked sixteen hours a day), centraliser of
power, spinner of meticulously intricate legal nets, promoter
of all kinds of state-owned or controlled industrial activities,
founder of the merchant navy, reformer of taxation, creator of the
'cadastre' (the register of all lands and their owners) and the
Bibliothèque Nationale. He gave the Académie, of which he was a
member, thirty-nine of its famous forty armchairs (one rich
'Académicien' had brought his own from home). This man was
the previously mentioned Jean Baptiste Colbert. There were two
such heroes in the last century alone, less than thirty-seven years
apart, an uncle and his nephew of the same name, Napoleon, the
former speaking French with a Corsican accent, the latter with a
German accent, both raised to power by the fear of the people in
moments of turmoil and danger. Philippe Pétain was the penultimate. De Gaulle, of course, was the last. At perilous times, the
French look for, to mention some examples, a victorious general
in the most recent war (Napoleon Bonaparte, Marshal Patrick
Mac-Mahon, duke of Magenta, first president of the Third Republic, Pétain, the defender of Verdun); or a restorer of central-
ised administration and rigorous finance (the two Napoleons,
Raymond Poincaré, Valéry Giscard d'Estaing). In war they want a
resolute, unflappable, and unstoppable leader like Georges

Clémenceau or Charles de Gaulle. No such man is always available, to be sure, and at times public opinion pins its hopes, 'faute de mieux', on some picturesque character such as flash-in-the-pan Pierre Poujade, a shopkeeper who stirred up masses of protesting taxpayers in the 1950s, or the poor general, Georges Boulanger (1837–1891), on his white charger, who seemed for a while in the 1880s a serious threat to the Republic but soon lost his prestige, his followers, and his nerve, and pathetically killed himself on the tomb of his recently dead mistress, Marguerite Crouzet Vicomtesse de Bonnemain, in the cemetery of Ixelles in Belgium.

These heroes of French history are proudly remembered and universally worshipped only after their deaths. When alive they all had an appalling time. Their job was always an ungrateful and dangerous one. They had to collect taxes, levy reluctant soldiers, defend themselves from dastardly plots, avoid being murdered, suppress mutinies and rebellions, and often fight bloody civil wars. Some of them were killed by assassins. Few Frenchmen really like a stern ruler, just as few people like bitter medicines. Nobody likes the impartial application of the law. Colbert died cursed by everybody, hated by Louis XIV, the king he had made great and powerful, and had to be buried secretly, at night, to avoid hostile demonstrators who might have snatched his body from the coffin and torn it to pieces. Louis Philippe was dethroned by a revolution in 1848 and fled, because his prudent despotism, his love of the 'juste milieu', common sense, and the lack of imagination had enriched France but bored the bourgeoisie. Obviously the French (like most people) love their country to be great and glorious but are reluctant to pay the price. 'Il faut payer pour être la France,' de Gaulle pithily warned them in vain more than once.

Unquote.   643 words

This passage is taken from The Europeans by Luigi Barzini. The chapter it is taken from is titled 'The Quarrelsome French'.

Estimating your reading speed

How to calculate your speed

This is the formula to apply for this quotation passage:

$$\text{Speed} = \frac{\text{No. of words in passage (643)}}{\text{minutes}}$$

Say you took 2 minutes and 35 seconds to read this passage.
2 min 35 sec = (2 + 35/60) = 2.58 minutes

$$\text{Speed} = \frac{643}{2.58} = 249 \text{ words per minute}$$

General formula

There is another way to assess your reading speed: this other approach is used when you read material that you have chosen, and you control the test reading time you wish to devote to it.

Speed or words per minute =

$$\frac{(\text{words per line}) \times (\text{lines per page}) \times (\text{pages read})}{\text{Time}}$$

If you use this formula, you should select a reading time in advance and stop when it has elapsed. Choose 1, 2, 5 or 10 minutes for your test read. Use an alarm clock to tell you when the set number of minutes have elapsed. If you stop reading three-quarters of the way down the page, divide your page into quarters. For example, if you have read three and three-quarter pages you have read 3.75 pages. If your passage has a lot of short lines, use your judgement to make up full lines, and estimate the fraction of a page that the words fill.

Comprehension

This book does not ask you to answer comprehension tests. Reading is an individual task. Your level of comprehension depends very much on your previous knowledge or familiarity with a subject and your ability to concentrate. You, the reader, are best placed to assess this. The questions to ask yourself about the passage you have just read (Barzini – 'The Quarrelsome French') to check your comprehension are:

■ Have I got the general idea of what this passage was about?
■ Is it sufficient for my present purpose?
■ Am I missing some of the details? If so does it matter?
■ Do I understand enough of what I have read, so far, to continue?

Thus comprehension is subjective, and the quality or level of your comprehension will vary according to what you read and your purpose in reading it. A flexible approach, which includes different reading speeds, will help you adapt to different comprehension requirements.

Good comprehension encompasses:

■ Being able to select and understand what you need
■ Retaining and recalling that information
■ Connecting this new information to existing knowledge

Selecting and understanding what you need is made easier by reading with an objective in mind. It will give you the freedom to abandon unnecessary detail without feeling guilty.

The more you use this new information the greater will be your long-term retention. A method for increasing your recall is developed in the next chapter.

To connect new knowledge with old ask yourself questions about the material you have just read and relate it to what you already knew. In this way, you modify, update and enlarge your knowledge consciously. You can also discuss the subject with others, or summarise it in a report. These methods involve you physically in the process of comprehension and are tests in determining whether the material has been assimilated correctly.

Checklist for recognising bad habits

Determining your reading speed is only one of the factors that you are evaluating. You possibly have other bad reading habits.

Do you agree with George Crabbe (1754–1832) who wrote:

'Habit with him was all the test of truth,

It must be right: I've done it from my youth.'

or with Marcel Proust (1871–1922) who wrote:

'The firmness of a habit is usually in proportion to its absurdity.' ('La constance d'une habitude est d'ordinaire en rapport avec son absurdité.')?

Habit is not taught but is acquired. Habit, as defined by the Oxford English Dictionary, is 'a tendency to act in a certain way acquired by frequent repetition of the same act'. There are two types of habits which we can relate to reading: good habits and bad habits; habits which help and reinforce efficient reading and habits which hinder efficient reading. Chapters 2 and 3 aim at replacing your negative habits with positive ones. Changing habits is no easy task. Habits are engrained deeply, and have become a part of your routine.

In the passage about the French that you read did you:

- Hear the words in your head as you read
  (subvocalised)?   yes   no
- Read one word at a time?   yes   no
- Go back and re-read because you lost the meaning?   yes   no
- Have problems remembering what it was about?   yes   no
- Experience difficulty in maintaining your focus on
  the page?   yes   no
- Find that your concentration wandered off?   yes   no

If you have more than one bad habit – the number of 'yesses' in the list above – list them in order of their severity for you and go to the chapters in this book that deal specifically with them. This book, like many books, gives you a lot of advice, much of which you do not need. Therefore read only those sections that you do need to make you a rapid reader. Practise skimming now.

2 Minimising bad reading habits: maximising positive ones

In this chapter . . .

Improving your reading ability requires a series of step-by-step exercises designed to eliminate the negatives in your reading behaviour and to accentuate the positives. In this chapter the bad habits common to many normal or poor readers are discussed.

They are:

- Over-checking your reading and subvocalisation
- Not eliminating procrastination and interruptions
- Letting stress overwhelm you when faced with too much to read or physical difficulties linked with reading, like dyslexia

You are told what the habit is, how it impairs your reading and how it can be cured. Next, the chapter develops those positive habits you need to build on or strengthen:

- Increasing your motivation
- Why you must concentrate
- You have memory – just train it to be better
- Your comprehension will now increase

When this chapter has been digested you will be ready to get down to the drill of improving your reading skill.

How to reduce subvocalisation

Subvocalisation is hearing the words in your head, or saying the words to yourself as you read them. All readers do this to some degree. It is a bad habit when it is frequent rather than occasional. Moving your lips when you read is the extreme form of subvocalisation. If you subvocalise frequently you need to understand why. When you learned to read, you said each word aloud to reinforce the relationship this particular order of letter conveyed as that word. Later, as you gained speed, reading aloud was discouraged. Some readers never lose this checking mechanism. They were not taught to modify their reading habits. They, particularly, were not taught to READ WORDS IN A GROUP, rather than singly. A fluent reader does not need to 'hear' the words to understand the meaning of what he reads.

Reducing subvocalisation is easy. You must understand that you can subvocalise only a limited number of words before it slows you down. If, for example, in the speed exercise of Chapter 1 you achieved a speed of 200 words per minute and you wish to double it, you have to drop some subvocalisation. You simply must force yourself to read faster. Then you won't have time to 'hear' the words. At first you may feel a little disoriented. You will feel that you do not understand what you are reading. But persevere and trust yourself!

As you gain speed, you will find that you are converting the sounds into pictures – as images. We have the ability to visualise. When reading and visualisation are combined, your speed and your comprehension are high. The text has become a slow motion movie.

To practise visualisation, start with simple words. When you see the word 'house', picture in your mind a house. As you get better at visualisation, words describing abstracts will literally become shapes, colours or pictures in the same way as concrete words. Then you will be reading using both sides of your brain as described in Chapter 1.

How to reduce procrastination and interruptions

Slow readers tend to put off reading as much as they can, for as long as they can. If you belong to this group you need to understand the reasons for your behaviour. It is because either:

1 You perceive reading as an unpleasant, long, tiresome task
OR
2 The material is complex and overwhelming and you do not know how and where to start. But these reasons for delay have to be overcome.

If you find reading unpleasant and tiresome, you can either:

1 Tackle it cheerfully, because it cannot be avoided
OR
2 Do it grudgingly, harming yourself in the process with negative feelings

If the material is complex and overwhelming, you need to follow these rules:

- Start as soon as possible. Remember the Chinese proverb: 'A 1000 mile march starts with the first step'
- Divide the material into chunks
- Take five minutes rest every twenty to thirty minutes. This makes the going easier and raises your concentration level
- Give yourself a pat on the back. Consider what you have already achieved. Tell yourself it's not **that** complicated. (That's why breaking into chunks is important.)
- Commit yourself to deadlines, and end your reading at the allotted time

Preparing for serious reading means getting away from the telephone. It means making it known to others that you are going to study a document and do not want to be disturbed. It could mean shutting your door or hiding in a quiet part of the house. Or having your secretary take the phone calls and discourage visitors for a while. As long as you do not isolate yourself too often and you return phone calls, people – on the whole – will respect this private time. Alternatively you could go to the office early or stay late. Perhaps a quiet hour at home before your work day starts is the answer. Whatever is best for you, develop a regular habit, to get through that material that piles up in your in-tray.

The above recommendations are simply common sense. But all of them are linked with efficient use of time and, thus, reinforce better reading habits.

How to reduce stress

All of us experience stress at times. But stress is subjective. What may be stressful to you, may not be so to someone else. In his book *Understanding Organisations* Charles Handy distinguishes between 'pressure' and 'strain'. Pressure can be beneficial and stimulating, when it helps us meet deadlines or increases our performance. Strain is damaging when we live daily with anxiety, fatigue, or harassment.

Some pressure is beneficial through brain and glandular processes as it stimulates the production of certain hormones, such as those of growth and adrenaline, which increase the metabolic rate of the body. The production rate of some other hormones is decreased. The hormone balance of the body is tilted to help the body achieve the task in hand. If this imbalance is short term, no harm is done. If the situation is prolonged over many days or weeks, damage, such as high blood pressure or lowered resistance to disease, may occur (see Winter and Winter, p. 93).

It is important that you analyse how stressful your life is. Make a list of things that cause you strain at work and at home. If you are plagued with a feeling that you are always fighting a losing battle – the 'one-damned-thing-after-another' syndrome – you will not be able to concentrate and absorb written material. The strain that you experience overwhelms the motivation. It reduces your flexibility and heightens your tension.

Improving your reading may be a way for you to reduce a stressful situation. If this is the case, you may have to help the process by changing your lifestyle. This change could take the form of meditation, more physical activity, or taking breaks at regular intervals, not only during the year but also as part of your daily routine.

Alvin Toffler found that managers thriving under pressure (stimulating stress) have developed 'stability zones'. For some, stability is found in the family, with a wife as an active partner. For others, it is the refuge provided by daily routines regardless of where they are; for example, reading, exercising or taking a nap at the same time every day.

How to reduce the effects of dyslexia

Most poor readers have nothing intrinsically wrong. They simply find acquiring reading skills more difficult than learning say, arithmetic or computer languages or music. However some poor readers have an emotional or medical reason for their learning difficulty with reading. Dyslexia simply means the learning difficulty caused by a medical problem. The term 'learning difficulties' covers symptoms caused by emotional or linguistic problems and a variety of medical causes. 'Specific developmental dyslexia' is used when the problem can be medically categorised, and it is usually diagnosed in childhood due to the obvious symptoms (see McAuslan, p. 93).

Much progress has been made in the past ten years towards an understanding of what dyslexia is but there is an enormous amount still to be learned and understood. Dyslexia can vary from a very mild form, only manifest during childhood, to a form which continues to cause substantial difficulties throughout life. Dyslexia may be a consequence of partial deafness when young, or be induced by emotional tension or some brain malfunction. It is unlikely that anyone with a substantial degree of dyslexia would read this book.

But what of the person who has not been diagnosed as having a learning difficulty or dyslexia, but who privately has to struggle hard to keep up with his contemporaries? How do you identify him?

First, there is the obvious evidence of difficulty in learning reading skills. Then there might be more specific symptoms of dyslexia including an inability to distinguish left from right, or confusing objects with their mirror images. This is called 'crossed laterality'. It is manifest, for example, by confusing 'b' with 'd', or confusing the spelling of 'from' and 'form'. People with severe dyslexia may read 'puppy' as 'small dog', or 'Belgium' as 'Holland' (see Anthony Smith, p. 93). The characteristics common to these pairs of words indicate that the brain makes many correct associations, but fails to select the single, correct, word at the end of the reading/visualising/recall process.

Other symptoms of dyslexia, which are not at all uncommon, include:

- ambidexterity
- lack of concentration
- clumsiness
- defective speech

But readers of this book are not likely to have these symptoms to a significant extent. However, many well-known people have displayed one or more of these symptoms and have successfully overcome the handicap.

It is best for someone with a significant learning difficulty to seek professional help. But if you suspect you may have a mild form you can help yourself to read faster by using a multi-sensory approach. You need to learn to read using, simultaneously, as many of your senses as possible. You acquire such a capability by drill. For example, here are a couple of very simple practices:

- The use of a guide – the finger or a pointer run vertically down the centre of the page at a reasonably fast speed – is one. The eyes are forced to follow the guide. This improves reading discipline and speed. (See Chapter 3 for details of 'pacers' to gain reading speed.)
- Moderately dyslexic persons sometimes have erratic eye movements. A very simple visual aid, to train the eye to move horizontally, may correct this problem. The aid is a window (slot) cut in the centre of a large postcard. The window is the shape and size of one line of print. As the window is run down the page, the eye is limited to horizontal movements since the window shows only one line at a time

Sensory assistance can help your reading in other ways. Link the read words (or groups of words) to as many sensory impressions as possible. Groups of words can be hooked on to images (little scenes described by the text) or your knowledge of the light, the sounds, the smells or touch of objects associated with the text you are reading. A young person may be helped if the observed scene is linked to reading. In the extreme, if a brown furry cat in the garden is crouching to catch a bird, the key words of this scene may be written down (possibly in brown ink), and by touching the cat (probably later), and smelling the garden (maybe the grass has been cut recently). In this way connections may be established between the words and other senses.

How to improve concentration

If you reach the bottom of a page and you do not remember what you have read, your concentration is poor. You have allcwed your mind to wander off; you have given in to distractions. External distractions can be greatly reduced if you minimise disruptions as was mentioned earlier. But reading and working in a noisy environment is quite possible when the mind learns to filter out the distraction. Another aid to concentration is to read at the time of day which suits you best; some people perform better in the morning, some late at night.

The environment in which you read and work is important. While daylight is easier for your eyes, any comfortable light, if it is not too bright nor too dull, is adequate. For body comfort, the temperature should be about 20 degrees Celsius (more for Americans!). However, most people's brains work better at about 18 degrees Celsius. The best posture for most people is one which puts a minimum of strain on muscles. Therefore a chair which supports your legs, particularly the thighs, comfortably, and allows you to lean forward slightly, is recommended.

To help you eliminate internal distractions – letting your mind wander off on to more attractive thoughts – model yourself on children. Children seldom concentrate on anything for long. But when they do, they get totally immersed in the task in hand. If fifteen minutes of reading at a stretch is all that can hold your interest, then so be it. Give it your best and stop as soon as your attention lapses. But as you leave the reading, summarise, on paper or in your mind, the essential points of what you have just read.

As you discover and develop your rapid reading ability, you will find that the most powerful way of avoiding internal distraction is to anticipate what you are about to read. A big help here is to start the reading by having an overall idea of the work. Treating a book as a whole, a key step in this, will be described in Chapter 4.

How to improve memory and recall

The ability to quickly grasp the overall contents and general idea of a document helps the reader to save time, and keeps him from becoming sidetracked and bored. The technique of skimming a document to pick up the idea of the overall contents is described in Chapter 3.

One key factor which hinders the quick comprehension of a document, and detracts from long term retention of new knowledge, might be called 'interference caused by subsequent learning'. New learning can interfere with the recall of material learned previously. The solution to this is 'chunking'. Arrange your reading and learning in time chunks of only one document or subject. Change documents or subjects only after a refresher period or after a different activity has been performed. This prevents knowledge of a new subject interfering with a subject learned earlier.

Psychologists have long known that retention of knowledge decreases with time, particularly if the knowledge is not revised, or used. The graph (Figure 2.1) illustrates how retention and recall ability decays. Recent researchers have demonstrated that, given the correct stimulus, we can remember everything. This shows that we retain perfectly what we do everyday; the problem starts when we try to retrieve or recall this information.

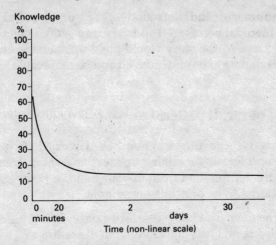

Figure 2.1 Knowledge recall ability versus time
Note that o time is the time when '100%' knowledge was acquired via sight,
sound, smell, touch or taste. After Hermann Ebbinghaus, about 1885.

Why do we forget? 'The easiest answer is, we don't.' writes
Professor J. Z. Young. We have many subconscious memories.
The problem lies in the fact that we have not yet mastered a
system for retrieving them. A clue to one retrieval technique is
provided by a man, the workings of whose extraordinary
memory has been documented (A. R. Luria, p. 93). 'S', a failed
journalist, could remember perfectly any nonsense list or mathe-
matical formula or other set of data, many years after it had been
given to him. 'S' innately used a system which was based on
incorporating or combining new data with the data he already
knew. He connected mentally or 'hooked', in his mind, the **new**
items to **old** familiar objects, making strong images, through
which he could recall the new data.

For example, when he was given a complicated formula, a part
of which was perhaps like

$$h = \sqrt{981}.F \times vm^2 \ldots$$

he would build a little story around it and facts in his past life.
Henry (h), an old friend, has given him a ruler (=) with which he

is going to measure the bare roots (√) of a tree. The tree is 981 cm high, but F(reda) is cross (×) and very mad (vm), in fact, doubly so (^{2}) . . . and so the story would build up, causing enormous quantities of data to be remembered and be retrievable.

The use of recall patterns

In reading we can use a system, as described above under Memory and Recall, for linking up ideas or areas of knowledge. To keep the information fresh in your mind, it helps if you use recall patterns.* The principles are simple:

■ Write the main idea in the centre of a page
■ Add associated ideas branching from the centre
■ Use keywords which summarise a train of thought
■ Write in capitals rather than script for legibility

Figure 2.2 is an example.

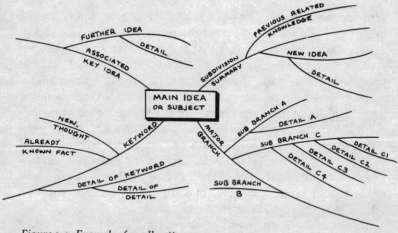

Figure 2.2 Example of recall pattern

Now, apply it to the passage we read about the Quarrelsome French. The example (below) is not the only way of summarising

*Tony Buzan calls them 'Mindmaps'.

the passage. To show how you connect old and new knowledge, the pattern has included assumed previous knowledge.

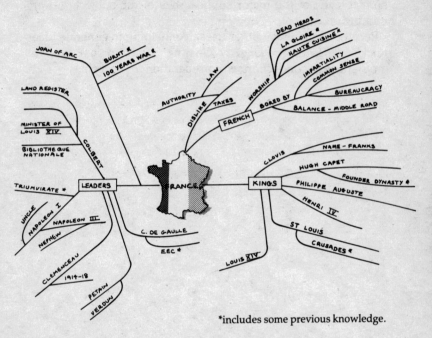

*includes some previous knowledge.

Figure 2.3 *Example recall pattern recording notes on France*

The advantage of recall patterns over linear notes is that you organise the notes yourself and do not have to follow the plan expressed by the author. Thus, it allows you to hook new pieces of information to old immediately, and it allows you to tailor the information to the emphasis that you, rather than the author of the book, require.

Should you have trouble, particularly at the beginning, in following your own structure, remember Kipling's poem:

I keep six honest serving-men
(They taught me all I knew);
Their names are What and Why and When
And How and Where and Who.

What, Why, When, How, Where and Who will guide you, if you have difficulties assembling your recall pattern, when you apply them to each of the major subheadings of the subject you are working on.

Recall patterns have other uses, like helping to generate ideas quickly. *Effective Speaking* by Cristina Stuart (p. 93) explains another use in connection with preparation for speeches.

3 Becoming a rapid reader –
a step-by-step approach

In this chapter . . .

You select a book and prepare for a series of exercises that
teaches you the technique of rapid reading. It is
recommended that you complete all the exercises in about
one hour. Each exercise is a step; there are seven in all:

- Initial reading speed exercise
- Motivation
- Overcoming regression
- Using peripheral vision
- Using a guide as a pacer
- Conditioning
- Consolidation

Each step is introduced by a description; you practise it
once: an analysis follows. First we improve eye movements
by reducing the number of **fixations**, then we increase
comprehension speed to match the reading speed.

Throughout all exercises keep a record of your speed and
comprehension. If your eyes get tired, do exercises to rest
them. Finally, there is advice on how to maintain and
increase the new reading speed you have reached.

Preparation for reading

This chapter shows you the technique for becoming a rapid
reader. To familiarise yourself with the material and to learn to

anticipate, browse through the whole chapter looking at the sub-headings, the diagrams and the summary at the beginning of the chapter. To work through this chapter, doing the exercises with a co-operative friend, should take about one hour.

Have a stopwatch or clock, a sheet of paper and a pencil by you. Set up the table (Figure 3.1) on the paper. Or use this table to record your progress.

Exercise	Speed	Comprehension
1 Initial reading		
2 Motivation		
3 Overcoming regression		
4 Peripheral vision		
5 Using a guide		
6 Conditioning		
7 Consolidation		

Figure 3.1 Results of reading exercises

Ensure that your lighting is comfortable. Minimise the possible interruptions. Choose a comfortable chair and place it by a table. (In some of the exercises below it is best if you have the help of a friend.)

Now, select a book. As we are going to learn a skill together, it is important that you choose a book that is interesting and light. Go for a novel; avoiding 'classics', or humorous books. You are going in the shallow end of the pool for a few exercises, before you plunge in the deep end. It is better to tackle the technique with a document that is easy to understand, rather than multiplying the difficulties by adding deep philosophy or strong humour.

New books, particularly paperbacks, should be 'broken-in'. A book that wants to shut all the time is not helping you to read it: the fight is rather off-putting. Place the spine of the book on the table. Open the book at regular intervals, starting roughly at page 30; with the palm of your hand press the book open several times along inside the spine of the book. Repeat every thirty pages or so, to the end. Do not open the book in the middle of bending the covers backwards to meet: it breaks the spine of the book and the pages will fall out soon.

We will proceed step by step, with a series of exercises to illustrate and practise each step. The overall objective is to make you a better reader. That will mean building on what you already know, and perhaps changing one or two of your past habits.

Now, think positively: you *can* read faster!

Initial speed

Set yourself a reading time: two, three or five minutes and set your watch. Start reading the book, as you do normally. When the time is up, make a mark with your pencil where you stopped and calculate your speed, using the formula given in Chapter 1. Record your speed on the table from Fig. 3.1. Also give yourself a mark between 0 and 10 to express your comprehension. This mark must reflect what YOU think you got from the reading. Do you have a good, general idea of what you read? Did you miss some bits, or have you forgotten them already? Is it important? Can you go on? Evaluating comprehension each time you do a reading test will give you a rough idea of your reading progress. We will work on comprehension in greater detail later.

The reading speed for the average English-speaking person is between 200 and 300 words per minute. If you are slightly below, let's say you are within the average. If you are above, you have a head-start. If you are very much below, you will have to pay attention to your faults and practise to correct them.

So, we are now equipped with an initial or reference reading speed which we are going to improve.

Motivation

Your objective now is to **double** your reading speed. Whatever you achieved in the first exercise, aim to double it. To encourage you to do this, let's play a game. Suppose that if you double your speed you will win a superb prize.

Now, take the book again, and start reading from the last pencil mark. Read for the same amount of time as you did for Exercise 1. Mark the book with the pencil where you stopped. Note your speed and comprehension at Exercise 2.

You must have achieved a higher speed than before, or, indeed, you have doubled your speed. You have experienced motivation. Motivation is the basic step that you have to apply every time you pick up something to read.

Poor readers lack motivation because their experience of reading has not been rewarded. To overcome this problem you need to:

■ Establish objectives
■ Read in SHORT bursts

Before you proceed with the other exercises, it will help you if you set an objective NOW. In future your objective(s) will be to concentrate either on the plot or the main character. After these exercises, when using rapid reading, you will search for all the facts about chemical x and its derivatives for example, or everything relating to current cost accounting methods. Decide on your objective and pay scant attention to everything else. Apply this principle now, with the novel you are reading.

My objective is: _____

Eye movements and regression

Ask a friend to sit opposite you about one metre away. Hold your book up, but so that he or she can see your eye movements over the book, while you read two or three lines. Ask your friend to describe the eye movements that he sees. You may also like to see your friend's eye movements when he reads. Your descriptions probably follow this diagram (see Figure 3.2):

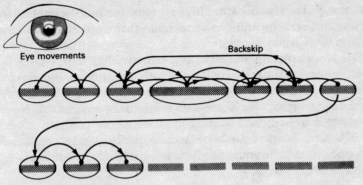

Figure 3.2 Eye movements

Each balloon represents the eye resting on a word or group of words. In this example the eye goes forward five times, skips backwards three spaces, then goes forward four more times.

That is, your eyes move with jerky movements or saccades, as they were first named. They take in a word, or group of words and recognise the shape of the letters; the brain recalls the meaning of the word, or words, then your eyes go on to the next word, and then to the next and at each word the eye-brain process takes place. Now, the eyes may **go back** to check what was read before – perhaps because it is a foreign name, or because the word is unfamiliar. Then the process starts again, until the eyes reach the end of line and then . . . zoom . . ., like a typewriter, the eyes start again on the next line.

Every time the eyes stop on a word, it is called a **fixation**. Untrained eyes will fixate six to eight times per line. Every time the eyes go back to check on a word, it is called **regression** or **backskipping**.

A fixation can last from a split second to one second in very slow readers. One of the first things that you must try to do is to reduce the number of fixations to, say, four per line. And the first principle you are to put into practice is to eliminate regression. This will help you to read smoothly. The smoother your eye movements, the faster you read.

Why do you regress? Because you are unsure of what you read and think that you have missed something important. That may be true, but it is inefficient. There are two possibilities: either it is important and the author will mention that word again; or it is not; so why worry about it?

As you go on and you pick up speed, avoiding regression will become easier: the speed will make you concentrate more; this in turn will heighten your overall comprehension and will encourage you to anticipate. Regression will become redundant. Now pick up your book and read for the same amount of time as you did before. Mark your book with a pencil where you have stopped. Calculate your speed and record speed and comprehension against Exercise 3.

Peripheral vision

Sit opposite a friend, about a metre apart. Have your friend hold his or her index fingers, tips touching each other, between your faces, at the distance from you where YOU normally hold a book. Your friend will now move his fingers apart, horizontally, slowly. **You** must look at his eyes, not his fingers. When one of the fingers goes out of your field of vision tell him to stop moving it. Do the same on the other side. Now look at the space between the two fingers. Repeat the exercise, with the fingers moving vertically. (See Figure 3.3.) You can determine your peripheral vision by yourself if you stare at **one** letter in a line of print. Place a finger on the letters each side of it. Then move the fingers apart until you can no longer recognise the recently uncovered letters. The distance between the fingers is probably wider than you had expected. It represents your peripheral vision. You use peripheral vision every day; when you drive, for example. Without moving your eyes, you notice that a light is changing colour, a child is about to run across the road, and so on. All the while you are concentrating and looking straight ahead.

When it comes to reading, however, you make little use of this peripheral vision if you look at only one word at a time. Focus your eyes on a particular word in a line of print, then try to read the words on either side. With training, you can 'take in' several words at a time (in one fixation) so that you now read as shown in Figure 3.4. Note that the eye focuses onto larger groups of letters

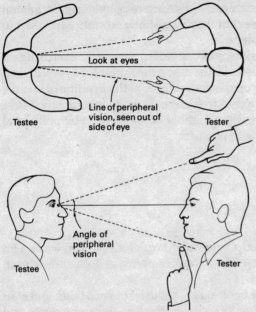

Figure 3.3 top: *Horizontal peripheral vision assessment*
bottom: *Vertical peripheral vision assessment*

or words than before. The eye goes to the centre of each 'balloon'
and uses peripheral vision to see the characters which fill the
distance between the centre and the edge of each balloon. Thus a

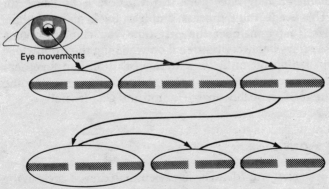

Figure 3.4 Eye fixations, using peripheral vision

few centimetres at each end of line are read by using peripheral vision, and now the eye is moving a shorter distance from left to right than it was before.

As peripheral vision is so useful it is worth exercising to improve it. Draw a vertical line down the middle of a page of text. Then, focusing only on the vertical line, at the first line of text see how many letters are seen to either side of the vertical line. Move down the vertical, and the number of letters seen by peripheral vision will increase with practice.

```
     a | c
    xy | zo
   mop | zag
  acts | uvwy
and so | on and
```

If you don't make peripheral vision work for you, you waste a lot of effort and energy reading blank margins, at both ends of each line!

So, now take your book again, at the last pencil mark and start reading, remembering to apply **motivation** (it can be done, and your objective), as well as trying to take in groups of words in one fixation. Read for the same time as before.

When you have finished this reading exercise, mark the book with a pencil to note where you stopped, calculate and record your speed at Exercise 4. Your speed may have gone down. Your comprehension may have gone down. There is no cause for alarm. This is a learning process, and learning is made of highs and lows. Just remember the first time you climbed onto a bicycle: you probably concentrated on watching the front wheel and kept falling off until, as if by magic, it all 'fell together', posture, movement, looking up straight, and you were speeding down the road, probably unable to stop and get off safely.

Using a guide

Sitting opposite your friend again, ask him to draw a circle in the air with his or her eyes, i.e. follow the circumference of an imaginary circle which may be around your head. Observe the eye movements and describe what you saw. Probably the eyes move following a shape like this:

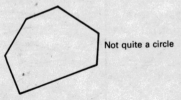

Not quite a circle

Figure 3.5 Unguided eye movements

Now, guide your friend's eyes with your finger, by drawing an imaginary circle in the air. Your friend's eyes follow the finger. Observe your friend's eyes again. Their movement now is smoother, like this:

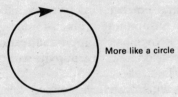

More like a circle

Figure 3.6 Guided eye movements

This suggests that, to help your eyes move **smoothly** on a page, to avoid wandering off and regressing, you need to guide your eyes when you read. Initially, the guide will take your eyes along each line, and down the page, line by line. This is something that you already do. If you are suffering from toothache you take the telephone book to look up the telephone number of your dentist. You use your finger to search down the column for the correct name and number. Why? Because you are in pain and are trying to save time as well as not wishing to make an incorrect call. You are motivated.

So, from now on, use a finger or the tip of a pencil as a guide – whichever feels comfortable when you read. A finger is recommended because usually you have it with you and thus you have no excuse for not using it while reading!

Figure 3.7 Using a finger as a reading guide or pacer

Let us put this into practice. Take your book again and start reading, for the same amount of time as before, starting at your last pencil mark. Remember to apply **motivation** – your **objective**, to avoid **regression**, and to **group the words** – fixating, say, 4 times or less per line.

Mark your book where you have stopped, calculate your speed and record both speed and comprehension at Exercise 5 – Using a guide.

Did your reading speed and comprehension go up? If they did, that is good. Move on to the next exercise. If you think the finger – or pencil – slowed you down, then move it faster in future!

You may also have found the guide a distraction, or that using it felt strange. Don't give up; persevere. You are not used to using a guide systematically, as you have just done. With practice, the guide will help you to gather speed and will focus your concentration.

Introducing rhythm

In Chapter 1 we explained that reading benefits greatly from use of the right side of our brain. This includes rhythm. Some people have an innate sense of rhythm and find it easy to apply. One way to start is to move along the lines following your heartbeats, so that your finger (or pencil) traces one line per heartbeat. Do this for a page or so.

Now try to increase the pace either by saying 'line', 'line', 'line' . . . to yourself, or by using a metronome set at a speed slightly faster than is comfortable. Do this for two pages, or until it feels natural.

Conditioning

We are now going to practise high speed reading with rhythm. You are going to read from your last pencil mark, using a guide and rhythm. Start at a comfortable pace and then progressively speed up until you cannot move your guide fast enough to keep up with the rhythm. At this point you will have to use a different motion with your guide. You will have to zig-zag down the page, tracing a maximum of three zig-zags per page.

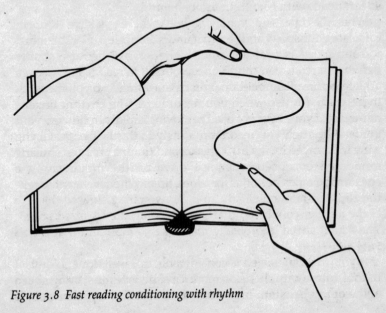

Figure 3.8 Fast reading conditioning with rhythm

To practise conditioning correctly, you need to handle your book correctly, with your left hand at the top of the right-hand page to turn the pages, while your right hand does the zig-zag movements, if you are right-handed. If you are left-handed and using your left hand as your reading guide, turn the pages with your right hand, so that the rhythm is maintained.

Set your watch for five minutes now and start from the last pencil mark. Remember that you are constantly speeding up, to end up by moving down the pages very fast, at the rate of about one per second. You may experience a blurr during the exercise. This is normal. Your eyes need to adjust to this new way of receiving and sending this information to the brain. To keep your motivation, start to look for keywords on each page. If you take in half a dozen words you are doing very well. Start now, and get hooked on speed!

Now, we are **not** going to record this speed. It was a practice exercise. Go back to your last pencil mark, the one you made at the end of Exercise 5. Set your watch for slightly **longer** than before and start reading, using all the techniques you have learnt so far. Read, with comprehension in mind.

When the time is up, mark your book where you have stopped, calculate your speed and record it under Exercise 6, Conditioning.

Your speed is probably a lot higher. Why? Because shortly before you read, you conditioned yourself to read faster. Like an athlete before a competition, you have warmed up your muscles to be ready for use when you need them. The rhythm became natural and your eyes got used to moving rapidly, following your guide. Although you read more slowly in this last exercise, you were influenced by the high speed conditioning. We are similarly influenced by speed when we drive on the motorway at a constant 70 miles per hour for a long time. When we want to take the sliproad marked clearly 40 mph, we rarely slow to this: we brake a little, convinced that we are doing the required speed. The actual speed is probably more like 50 mph and that seems very slow!

If your reading speed is considerably up, well done. Now, let us look into comprehension more carefully: we must bring **speed** and **comprehension** into **unison**. If your comprehension is

adequate, skip the next few lines and go on to the next exercise.
   If your comprehension is low, let us check a few things:

- Are you clear about your objective?
- Do you keep this in mind while you read?
- Do you move your guide smoothly underneath the lines of your page?
- Do you look for keywords along each line?

If you answer 'yes' to all this, then slow down. At this stage, there is no point in having speed for speed's sake.

If your answer is 'no', then pinpoint where you are going wrong and alter your habit. Then repeat the last exercise.

The speed used in the conditioning exercise is the speed you will apply when you overview a document quickly; this is described in Chapter 4. It is important that you understand the value of conditioning; practising zig-zagging to enhance your concentration and speed. Once you have experienced this several times, it becomes a habit and a necessary step to recognising quickly what you need in a document. It is only when you have mastered conditioning that you can claim to read faster and read with flexibility: High-speed to overview and a more leisurely speed – a cruising speed – to read what really interests you.

Consolidation

Take your book and begin to read at the last pencil mark. Read to consolidate everything we have learned so far. We are now trying to bring speed and comprehension together. Read for at least five minutes.

When the time is up, mark your book where you have stopped, calculate your speed and record it under Exercise 7, Consolidation.

Your reading should be more stable now. You have **motivation**, you have an **objective**, you are eliminating **regression**, you are **grouping** the words, you are using a **guide** to help you focus and concentrate, you can **speed up**.

If you still have difficulties, which is not uncommon at this stage, repeat exercises where you find difficulty. Learning a skill is unpredictable: some wonder why they did not take it up sooner, others stumble here or there and take a little longer. Remember you only started to read faster a few hours ago; all this is new and you are changing some habits that have been with you for many years.

Rest your eyes

You may have found these exercises tiring for your eyes or you may experience tired eyes without trying to read faster. Here are two exercises to rest your eyes.

Put your elbows on a table. Shape your hands into small cups in which you are going to rest your eyes. The word 'rest' is important. Do not apply pressure to the eyeballs as this would make the exercise useless. You should feel comfortable.

Close your eyes and create a picture. Imagine that you are standing in a large golden-yellow cornfield. It is a sunny summer day. Look all around you. Look to the left. There is a tall poplar rising to the sky. Look at it from the trunk up; look at the green leaves against the blue sky. In the sky, on the right there is a plane cruising from the right to the left. Now look at your feet, there are poppies, bright red poppies and in the distance, far away, on the right there is a church spire that rises on the horizon. Look at the whole scene again, the golden-yellow corn, the tall green tree, the blue sky and the plane moving from right to left, the poppies at your feet and the church spire in the distance. Remember that all this should have been done without feeling any pressure on your eyes.

When you take your hands away and open your eyes, things around you are much brighter and your eyes feel refreshed.

Another simple exercise is to focus on a far point – ideally out of a window. Hold the position for two or three seconds and then, without moving your head, focus on the nearest point in the room and maintain your focus for two or three seconds. Repeat the exercise five times.

Both these exercises require that you move the muscles that

surround your eyes. You move them sideways and up and down. It helps to keep your eyes in good shape. Visualising colour in the dark also has a restful effect. These exercises do not take long and are particularly beneficial if you work in artificial light (see references – W. H. Bates).

Maintaining your speed

When you feel that you have mastered the techniques of reading faster while maintaining comprehension (and it may take a little longer than doing the seven exercises), how do you keep your new skill?

To keep this newly acquired skill, you need to practice about five minutes every day. I am reminded here of the famous words of a ballerina: 'If you do not practise one day **you** notice it, if you don't practise for two days, the **public** notices it!' The practice takes the shape of high speed conditioning. The best material to practice on is a newspaper, because it has narrow columns and therefore you need only one fixation per line. Also, as a rule, a newspaper article, such as a leader, summarises a situation with which you are familiar already. It is easy to be fast, until you read new information or opinion, at which point you will slow down, but still keep a fast rhythm.

You may also be wondering, how fast should I read? There is no limit. It is what **you** feel is comfortable that is the norm. Remember that flexibility is synonymous with rapid reading, and that to get at what you want quickly is as important as reading and absorbing the information.

If you wish to go faster still, start the process again, in a step-by-step manner, as we have done through this chapter, focusing on speed first and comprehension later.

4 Reading a book

In this chapter . . .

We have learned the dynamics – the techniques – of reading faster. Now we are going to apply them, through six systematic steps. These steps are:

■ Recall. What do you know already about the subject?
■ Objectives. Set some before you start.
■ Overview. Get acquainted with the whole document.
■ Preview. Reject the irrelevant or what you know already.
■ Inview. In-depth reading of new material.
■ Review. Make a recall pattern of notes.

Documents have to be treated as a whole, and approached as you would a jigsaw puzzle competition. This analogy is explained, together with the importance of recall pattern note-taking and adopting a **flexible** approach to rapid reading. Examples to illustrate the systematic approach follow in the next three chapters.

Treat a book as a whole

Learning is a process of pattern building. New bits of information or knowledge are significant when they fit patterns already in your mind. Our collections of patterns are what we call education and experience.

When we see a pattern we do not relate to right away, we are disoriented. If we are inquisitive, we invent an explanation that fits. If we are not, or are preoccupied, we do not register the pattern. Take the picture as an example. The dots probably have no meaning for you. However, once you know that a Dalmatian dog is in the picture, you are able to find it since we all have a pattern for a Dalmatian dog.

Figure 4.1 What pattern fits this picture?

Books have patterns, too. The pattern is obvious in fiction, where a story-line is built around a hero and you follow him through various exploits and sub-plots. This concept of pattern is what is meant by 'wholeness'. The author had a plan and your first task for any reading material you consider – a book, a report, an editorial or newspaper article – is to discover the author's plan. Rapid reading of a book requires you to refer to and consider the material as a whole, to consider that book's plan – and you must know that plan!

The jigsaw puzzle analogy

Imagine that you are taking part in a jigsaw puzzle competition. The prize for winning, by being the first person to complete the picture, is £20,000. You are determined to be the winner. You have been practising solving jigsaw puzzles. Now you are in a large room with the other competitors. Each competitor is sitting at a table on which there is a sealed brown bag containing a jigsaw puzzle and its picture. At a signal, everyone starts.

What is the first thing you do? Recall your experience of solving jigsaw puzzles. Then, you tear open the bag and look at the picture. How long do you look at it? Not very long; probably a few seconds. Why? Because time is precious and because you do not need, at this early stage, to clutter your mind with details. All you want now is the general appearance, an overview of the picture. You have now fixed a target. It is a more essential step than you realise; otherwise, you start blind, unsure of the final objective.

Next, you empty the bag and arrange the pieces coloured side up. As you do this, you set aside the corner and straight-edged side pieces. You are going to make the border first because it is easily recognised and it has a limited number of pieces.

Next you make piles of pieces of a specific colour or pieces which have some distinctive pattern on them: a blue pile, or a pile of pieces having a black line across them, for example, and so on. Pieces that are difficult to attribute are left on the side, to come back to later.

You have already started to put the picture together, beginning with the corner pieces and straight edges. You go on to pattern blocks and colour blocks. If there are strange pieces, you do not spend too long with them but put them aside with the other piles of 'difficulties'. You will deal with them when the picture is more complete.

The way you are working gives you the best possible chance of being amongst the winners. You have:

- motivation (to win the prize, to be best)
- an objective (to complete the picture)
- well-defined chunks of concentration (sorting all the pieces

roughly, then finding the straight and corner pieces, and on to the colours)
■ postponed problems until it is easier to find a solution for them (putting aside awkward pieces for later)

The jigsaw puzzle approach should be applied to all reading material.

The systematic approach to reading

You have a book to read. These six steps are the systematic approach to reading a book.

1 What do I know?

Purpose

This is a warm-up exercise, similar to that carried out by an athlete before a competition. It also helps the reader to start to identify gaps in his knowledge.

Method

Consider the title and jot down a few keywords describing what you know about this subject. This memory search puts you in a positive mode and prepares you to connect new information to the knowledge you already possess. People sometimes say that they know nothing about a subject. This is rarely true. With the wealth of information people are bombarded with through the media, through travel, through conversation, is there anything so completely and utterly new that one's mind is an absolute blank? Remember what was said in Chapter 1: 'Reading faster is first an attitude'. This positive attitude starts here. As in the jigsaw puzzle competition, we get set to win the prize. We gain motivation.

Timing

This step should be done quickly, spending no more than two minutes.

2 Set objectives

Purpose

An analysis of your objectives increases your concentration and helps you to achieve them. It also boosts your confidence and helps you speed up.

Method

This **most important** step – establish your objectives – applies to all reading material. 'What are you reading it for?' This seems obvious. Yet those who complain that they do not 'get on' with reading, or that they have to read every word, or that they get bored, do so because they did not spend a few minutes establishing their personal objectives. It is the corner-stone that makes your reading more efficient and memorable.

'A man without a goal is like shooting a gun without a target' said Benjamin Franklin. The same analogy applies here. If **you** don't know what you are looking for, how can **you** find it? A book, particularly a textbook, contains a lot of information. It caters for a variety of people and the author does not know who his readers might be. So he develops some basic ideas, and links these to more sophisticated ones. It is the reader's job to choose what he needs and to concentrate on those parts, leaving the rest aside.

When you establish your objectives, trust your own existing knowledge and feel confident.

How do you set objectives? By formulating one, two or three questions. Questions force you to look for answers and help you to keep focused. For example, when you began to read this book, the questions you asked yourself might have been:

■ Will this book help me to read rapidly long office reports?
  or
■ Will I be able to read fiction twice as fast?
  or
■ Will I be able to stop moving my lips when reading?

Again, you must ask yourself what you want – do you want to improve your reading or information absorption ability? Is it a familiarisation with the subject, is it a deep understanding of the ideas, or a reinforcing of your knowledge that you seek? To return to the jigsaw puzzle analogy; we now know what the picture looks like.

Be specific when you set out your questions. Avoid all-embracing phrases such as 'get an awareness of', or 'acquire knowledge about', which is a common mistake among poorly motivated readers. Focus each question on a clear topic.

Timing

Don't set yourself unreasonable tasks. No more than five minutes.

3 Overview

Purpose

This gives you a feel of the book. You start to locate the information you seek and you decide whether the book is worth reading.

Method

Using the high speed conditioning learned in Chapter 3, do an overview of the whole book. Pay attention to whatever stands out. This will include the cover, the table of contents, the index, the introduction, the summaries, the tables, diagrams, illustrations, chapter headings and bullets (■) it contains. Flick through it very rapidly. This is not reading in the ordinary sense, but looking at the structure, presentation and contents of the book. You are starting to sort out the jigsaw puzzle pieces.

Timing

Take five minutes for this exercise, literally flicking through the pages.

4 Preview

Purpose

Preview keeps you focused. It is the art of rejection and keeps you from becoming sidetracked and distracted.

Method

Strike out, using a pencil, those parts of the document that do not help you meet your objectives. It also means rejecting repetition, padding or information that is already familiar. A glance, looking roughly four lines at a time, tells you whether a paragraph, a page or even a whole section contains the information you are seeking. It is not easy to do, as we are reluctant to actively disregard what someone has written. But it is essential if you are to keep to your objectives. When you hesitate, look again at the objectives. Be ruthless in eliminating whatever is not relevant. When your objectives are well defined, it is easy; with practice, it comes naturally. You are making piles of those jigsaw puzzle pieces which you think will be easy to do first.

Timing

Again, as quickly as you can. The time will vary with the type of material, the way it is presented and according to how well you defined your objectives. A typical time for a book might be ten minutes.

5 Inview

Purpose

Inview provides you with detailed understanding.

Method

You have identified the points that interest you. You are focused and ready to read in depth. Read with **comprehension** in mind. Read line by line. If you have problems with comprehension, keep going: the answer may be on the next page. Continue to treat the material as a whole, building up knowledge as you read.

Your speed will depend on the nature of your book. It is important to keep a flexible approach. Use a pencil or highlighter to mark key ideas or keywords. Now is the time to apply the rhythm and cruising speed we learned in Chapter 3. Try to keep a good speed, a 'tempo'; that is, you are moving along comfortably, but under slight pressure.

If, at the end of this in-depth reading, you have gaps in your comprehension, read the book again. It is surprising how much better comprehension and retention are if you read, rapidly, the same material two or three times rather than slogging through once, stopping at every difficulty. So, when you have a problem, make a mental note or mark the page and continue. Return to the problem later, if necessary. Inview is like assembling the edges and easy parts of the jigsaw puzzle.

Timing

Set yourself a realistic time for this task and stick to it. In steps one to four you cut out a lot of unnecessary reading. Now you can be generous (20–30 minutes) to ensure achieving your objectives.

6 Review

Purpose

To check that all objectives are met.

Method

To consolidate what you have read, you must link it to your previous knowledge. Make a recall pattern as we did in Chapter 2. This enhances long-term memory because you hook new information onto what you already know. It is also early use of this new material which means that it will become part of your knowledge. Review is also a way to check whether any fuzzy areas remain, which you may need to go back to briefly, later.

The recall pattern is the way to summarise and link ideas. You can refer to your book, or you can do it from memory.

Timing

Depending on the amount of detail, a typical time for one book may be ten minutes, but you may need longer.

Why wait until the end to make notes?

Make notes at the end of all the reading steps. This keeps you selective about the information you need to keep.

Do not make notes from the text as you read. These notes will reflect the sequence of ideas as you read them. It is inefficient because:

- It is time-consuming
- The notes will be unnecessarily bulky
- It encourages mental laziness
- It does not indicate that you are absorbing what you read
- The notes may not be necessary.

Notes made after the different readings contain what the document means for you. It is now part of **your** mental property or knowledge. To ensure long term retention of it, you need to link it to what was already in your memory. In order to do this, you will probably use a different lay-out or sequence from that used in the book because the information is yours and fits into your experience.

Also, writing and reading are two different activities, requiring different mental and physical actions. When they are mixed, each one interrupts the other as you go back and forth between them. When they are separated, they reinforce each other.

Flexibility in reading

'There is no one right way,' wrote Peter Drucker. What is true in management in general is true for the acquisition of a skill like rapid reading. Although we have been through a systematic approach to the reading of books, there are differences between individuals and between the documents they handle. Some steps can be omitted. We are going to have a look at several specialised reports and put this assertion to the test.

Rapid reading is like learning to cook. First you get the rules straight. You must acquire some basic principles like how to cook green vegetables or red meats; then you refine this knowledge with the elements for simple sauces. Once you have *got the basics*, and *understand why* things are done this way, you can *adapt* any recipe to your own taste, what feels right for you. So, you must follow the rules until they become second nature. When that stage is reached, you can skip a stage, or combine two, just as you would with your favourite dishes. Add more salt or substitute the cream to suit your needs and the ingredients that are available.

Summary of the six steps

These six steps are the systematic approach to rapid reading. Make sure you know and understand them. They are the tools needed to apply the dynamics – the personal reading technique or skill – learned in Chapter 3:

- Recall your previous knowledge of the subject
- Establish your objectives: select up to three
- Overview: pick up the document and get acquainted with it
- Preview: reject irrelevant and familiar material
- Inview: read carefully any new information
- Review: make recall pattern notes to link new and old knowledge.

Above all – *be flexible*.

5 Applying rapid reading to reports

In this chapter . . .

> Reprinted below is a report on project procedures. We are going to read it according to the method described in the preceding chapters. We will proceed through the six systematic steps that have been explained.
>
> At the end of this report you will find each step examined, explaining how one person may apply rapid reading to it. Obviously these notes are only one way of tackling the report. There are many other different 'correct answers' that could emerge as a result of other people, with different view-points and knowledge, reading it for different purposes. Remember to be flexible!

Management Tools – Project Planning Procedures

by A. K. Redway MSc., CEng., CChem., MBIM

Introduction

This article describes procedures for managers to use to undertake a project and how to control the necessary activity once it is initiated. In order that the manager can ensure the smooth running of all activities through to a successful conclusion, he must use the manpower at his disposal to the best effect, commit the financial resources available economically and meet the necessary time deadlines. This requires a significant effort in planning. The better prepared he and his staff are, the greater are the chances of the project reaching a profitable conclusion.

The following sections of this article deal with the typical elements required to make a plan, and with those factors which have to be considered and controlled in order that future activities take a predetermined course leading in the desired direction. Each one of these elements should be written up as one or more procedures to define the project for all management and staff concerned, so that all understand the background to the project, its objectives and their responsibilities to it.

The Plan

All other factors being equal, the man or company that succeeds makes fewer mistakes than the competition. The process of doing more things correctly can be planned. It is difficult to make provision for unforeseeable factors, but contingency items can be inserted into a plan as a precaution against unexpected changes in direction.

In planning a strategy, very broadly, all normal commercial business activities may be divided into routine daily activities (repetitive paper processing or production of goods, for example) or one-off unusual exercises (a company take-over or the construction by a company of new office buildings or factories for itself). Whichever type of activity a company engages in it requires the tools to do the job – the planning,

objectives, organisation, schedule, reporting procedures and controls to monitor achievement progress and financing.

Among the best of tools to organise or plan purposeful activities are procedures which may be written and published to appraise all staff of the plan.

The Procedures

During the initial weeks of the scoping of a scheme or project, amongst the many items requiring definition are the management methods by which the objective will be realised. These are the administrative or organisation guidelines to be followed, as opposed to legal, political or technical requirements. The management plan envelops and co-ordinates all other requirements so that, at the appropriate times, all parties who have a necessary input to the total process make their contribution towards the end product.

In general terms the main subjects dealt with in a project scope and procedures manual should be, typically:

■ Project purpose or objectives;

■ Job scope or size;

■ Basis of feasibility;

■ Division of responsibilities;

■ Responsible personnel;

■ Organisation chart and job descriptions;

- Financing arrangements;

- Agreements – contracts;

- Schedule – programme;

- Administrative arrangements and plan of execution;

- Cost and progress reports and controls;

- Legal, planning and insurance, and

- Implementation or construction.

During the initial conceptual phases of a scheme the above headings may represent proposed ideas, future developments or plans. Then, during the progression from propositions to actual confirmed plans, the manual will evolve into a firm working document, with actual facts recorded under the appropriate headings, which will have been modified to fit in with the firmed-up arrangements or job progress.

Most of the subjects listed above require a written procedure or instruction describing what has to be done. These procedures should be specified in such a manner that all staff on the job work together in a consistent co-ordinated manner. New personnel coming on to the job can soon find out how to do their duties, without disruption to the surrounding organisation.

The Project Objectives

First of all a definition of the end product or objective is required,

whether it is the production of a banking service or a new petro-chemical plant. Undoubtedly, during the attainment of the objective, changes will occur in both the end product and the method of reaching it. Flexibility is an essential ingredient of planning, execution and achievement, but only necessary cost-effective modifications should be introduced. Also simplicity is a wholly desirable quality of all procedures and objectives; it is only too easy to swamp essentials in masses of peripheral data or methods which detract from the most effective manner of execution.

> **Flexibility is an essential ingredient of planning . . .**

Between the conception of the idea and its realisation there lies, amongst many other activities, the creation of a concise, simple and clear set of procedures for the accomplishment of all essential activities. (Any other activities should be carefully reviewed for relevance and stopped immediately if not positively productive. If relevant, they should be incorporated into the procedure.)

The first activity, the definition of the work scope, may serve several functions. It may be used as the basis for economic and technical studies and for the evaluation of customer, staff and other sociological reactions. It can be used to initiate financing activity or stimulate interest in the planned development from political or local community groups, and, most importantly, interest the ultimate consumer or customer-representative bodies.

The project purpose or objectives section of the project scope manual is a concise description of what is to be created and for what purpose. It may also mention briefly the personnel involved, the time frame, the cost, location, size of facility, etc. It must be kept concise for people to understand the whole scope of the project quickly. Subsequent sections of the manual go into detail. The first of these is the job scope.

The Job Scope

The job scope or size is not only the numerical description of the magnitude of the job. It differs from the project objectives as it includes a list of all activities that have to be performed, such as planning, financing, construction, etc, for the completion of the objectives. It may list tasks which will be performed by other organisations. Besides describing the job scope required in order to reach the objective, it should describe briefly the objective – the end product – itself. This assists in evaluating the size of the task to be performed.

The Basis of Feasibility

Without proving the basis of the project's feasibility, time is wasted. It has to be shown on paper that the objectives are politically, socially and physically possible. Can land be acquired? Is there a real need for the project? Will trade unions accept it? The potential financing for the project has to be described, with the economic justification for it. What will be the return on the investment? Will the product be required by the market?

Division of Responsibilities

The division of responsibilities defines the split of work between the client and the contractor. In a more detailed form, it lists work scope and activities items against the individual department or organisation responsible for carrying them out. It is a precursor to job descriptions, and is essential, acting as a checklist, so that all participating personnel know their duties and all major task requirements are undertaken.

The Responsible Personnel

The organisation structure, job descriptions and responsible personnel are closely related sections which may be described together. Personnel have to be nominated to carry out various phases and activities of the job. Working relationships have to be defined by the organisation structure, and the personnel assigned to specific functions have to know what their jobs and responsibilities are by means of their job descriptions. Job descriptions are closely related to the scope and nature of the project; all activities to be performed must be allocated within the organisation – even those that will ultimately be sub-contracted to outside organisations – all of which will require administration from the project's central organisation.

Organisation Chart and Job Descriptions

In order to make clear 'who does what, and to whom', an organisation chart is an indispensible aid. This will show in a tree or pyramid diagram the branches and relationships between the head of the organisation and subsequent layers of managers and administrators down to the clerical or manual levels.

It is most important that lines of responsibility are clear – who reports to whom, who is responsible for what. Bearing in mind the very rough guideline that one leader can effectively control the work of a limited number of staff, the organisation splits downwards at each level into teams of five to ten staff. Each team should foster a co-operative spirit, not only internally within the team, but co-ordinating with surrounding teams. This should

apply whether the work is organised in matrix management or in-line departmentally.

In a matrix organisation everyone has a supervisor responsible for the job or project of the moment. The staff member and supervisor need not be members of the same department, skill, profession or trade, but they have been assigned by their departments to work together on the current job, usually in a task force formed specially for the project. They are usually full-time on one project only. This is the best organisational method to use to pursue a special project.

Departmental in-line organisation does not usually involve a task force and projects are processed through each department possibly with no single person taking a special interest in any particular project. In departmental organisation priority projects may founder.

The in-line structure is simpler but less flexible in meeting varying workload patterns and priorities. It is more suitable for the smaller organisation, each person has only one supervisor, who is responsible for both work quality and quantity. Any staff member may work simultaneously on two or more jobs, with perhaps better time availability utilisation, but inferior priorities and lines of communication, as other people working on the same job, may be physically located elsewhere.

Job descriptions serve several purposes. The principal benefits derived from formalised descriptions are that the duties of staff positions are made clear and thus the organisation is strengthened. The description should include the position, title, supervisor and subordinates, a list of duties, experience and educational requirements of the position incumbent. Recruitment for the position is tremendously improved. To the description can be tied accounts and personnel activities, such as salary band.

Financing Arrangements

The present-day complexity of financing arrangements renders it advantageous for key members of most job organisations to be aware of them. The terms and conditions under which a project proceeds can have an enormous influence on the job objectives and how they are attained. Many agencies from the World Bank through to local businesses want to attach conditions to money supply which will direct the ways in which certain activities are carried out. It is best if all these conditions are clarified early on in the job so that the money supply is not prejudiced. Typical restraints can include activities having to be carried out in a certain place, by a specified time, with certain staff, with goods being supplied by nominated vendors, etc. To add to the complexity of the situation there is increasingly restrictive

legislation which may prohibit a condition, particularly when jobs cross international boundaries.

In certain circles the awareness of the realities of economics are becoming increasingly rare. However, ultimately they come home to roost. Therefore it is imperative that the profitability of a venture is recognised and pursued, and any deviations from the plan are recognised and corrected. To this end certain aspects of the financing arrangements should be made known so that the project is set up with real economics within the objectives. This will mean that key activities are tailored to fit into the economic requirements of the objectives, and that the job will be successful.

Agreements

No present-day project of any size can proceed without a multitude of permissions and agreements. It is advisable to present an extract of agreements with other parties which affect basic items in the execution of the project. Thus, it can be assured that important aspects of agreements are produced properly into the necessary activities of the job. Factors can affect legal, labour, financial, economic, territorial and technical aspects of the job.

Client and partners have a deep commitment to the job. Ensure that their interests are properly protected as good business ethics and the contract or agreement require.

Licence and royalty agreements are common in business today. Many projects are totally dependent on them. They should be entered into very carefully and it should be made clear, in the project procedures, what they are so that they are dealt with in the correct manner. Frequently such agreements impose restraints on the licensee, which must be met if they are party to a contract.

Sub-contracts, in which services are procured from outside parties, are an essential component of all projects. Procedures for acquiring and administering sub-contracts should be carefully formulated and followed. If, in the course of the project, one's own company is providing services to an outside party, the scope of services should be carefully monitored to ensure conformance with the contract.

The Schedule

Time is money and it therefore pays to plan in advance a realistic programme for the development of the project's organisation and its realisation. A little foresight will eliminate the majority of foreseeable future problems.

There are many different activities to be planned and many different ways in which the schedule can be generated. The first or master schedule to consider is that for the overall job, from the present through to the full operation of the facility or service. This will cover the mobilisation of the required organisation, the preparation of the job documentation, the acquisition of equipment or services and the actual setting-up or building of the facility or service.

The master schedule may be presented as a time-scale bar chart or a very simplified activity-node network, or combinations or variations of these. Undoubtedly the best to use is the one most suitable or comprehensible to the users. (An excellent 'management presentation' schedule is the timescale bar chart, milestone or flag type. Here the termination of each discrete phase or activity is highlighted with a little flag. Planned and actual progress can easily be compared.)

Schedules may be drawn simply by hand, or better still put on a computer. Highly complicated networks with hundreds of activities and restraints can be quickly revised and updated periodically or whenever new knowledge is gained about the time span of an important activity.

In order to check a simple master schedule it is necessary to break it down into phases, for example, mobilisation, documentation, acquisition and construction. Then each of these is broken down further, obtaining advice from the specialists in these areas into tens, hundreds or even thousands of activities which are given time durations and start restraints by preceding activities. The degree of breakdown, which should be minimised, depends on many obvious factors. Only important factors should be considered.

Planning many aspects of the job springs from the schedule. Some of the principal items are:

- Manpower requirements;

- Budget allocations/cash flow;

- Latest dates for decisions or activities;

- Job progress requirements, and

- Job controls/reports requirements.

The schedule and cost budget should be developed for maximum economy, whilst maintaining the ultimate objective of the job fully. The job scope, schedule and budgets stand by the references against which actual progress may be measured and from which any necessary modifications or corrections may be planned.

Administrative Arrangements and the Plan of Execution

'Plan of Execution' is a term often used to describe the activities to be performed – how, when and by whom they will be performed – in a project being carried forward from the first to final activities in the overall job schedule. The administrative arrangements will have to be made around the plan of execution. They will define the details.

Probably the key to the execution plan is the type of organisation set up to execute the job. It may be organised departmentally, or by a special task force. The departmental organisation is effective if the job is not large, if all the different departments are properly manned for their work loads, and staff work best by staying in the same physical location continuously. However, a matrix staffed task force is indisputably better for a project with strict time and budget restraints set on it.

After choosing the type of organisation, it is necessary to decide how a large job will be staffed up and activity initiated. During the course of the job, the organisation will change. Initially it progresses through departmental contributions, grows into a full-scale task force and then shrinks at the end, unable to support enough personnel for a task force, back to a low level of departmental input.

A plan of execution concentrates consideration of the method of accomplishing a job. The head of the organisation to carry out the job must be appointed and he has to assemble, and coordinate, in one form or another, the team or personnel to assist him with the job. All these people (or the senior responsible people in each department) need to be named, and their relationships and duties in the team have to be defined by an organisation chart and job descriptions or functions.

The services to be provided, when, where, how and by whom, all need stating. A description of the sequence of events as the milestones of an objective schedule (or programme) are passed helps to clarify the future requirements and planning.

Writing a job scope and procedure, containing detailed administrative procedures, follows naturally from the plan of execution, giving the detail, whilst the plan is written in broad terms only. The basis of all aspects of the future work must be defined, together with the objectives, estimates, schedules, meetings and products.

Under administration it is possible to list many activities which have to be performed, such as control of communications, decisions, cash flow, design, procurement, dealing with outside entities, travel, etc. Such a list will ensure that each department or function is aware of the requirement, and fulfils it. If the activities are complex or repetitive it is best if the methods of performing the required work are described carefully so that as the work is completed it may be checked (and corrected) against a standard.

Cost and Progress Reports and Control

A report describes past history from which we should learn.

Control is the feedback of deviation followed by corrective action.

The carrying out of any job economically on schedule and within budget requires adequate, but not excessive, reports for management at all appropriate levels of the organisation structure. All members or teams of an organisation need to know what their work objectives are, and whether they are reaching them. Thus produced work has to be measured against scheduled work, against the time schedule and against the cost or man-hour budget. The comparison of actual and planned figures shows deviation which is then used in corrective action feedback.

Reports can be made in many forms. The best are simple and concise. The currently reported figures, whether on schedule or not, should be reviewed. Is the schedule too long or too short? Are manpower resources throttling the rate of progress, or is the job overmanned? However well or badly the job is progressing, the schedule – on which most controls are based – can be updated continuously and quality improved. By correcting for historical accuracy, the accuracy of the future forecast can be improved.

The majority of controls must, at any point in the time duration of the job, be converted into rates – or the total quantity charged to date – to be meaningful. Thus one of the best presentations of controls on generalised items or parameters, such as those listed below, is in the form of planned and actual curves plotted against time.

- Cash flow, budget committed;

- People, staff on the job, man hours expended;

- Products produced, drawings, documents, items of whatever the product is, and

- Consumption of raw materials, feedstock (which can include cash and time).

Any of these items may also be presented in a numerical tabular form.

Naturally it is most important to choose the minimum numbers of the most important parameters to monitor, or control, the job. The analysis of each parameter costs a lot of time and therefore the minimum number for proper control should be monitored. Also it is essential to analyse only those that are relevant or show what needs to be known in the simplest or quickest manner. Irrelevant statistics are a menace.

Further useful analysis can be made by checking the ratio of production numbers against the consumption of raw materials. This gives a 'materials efficiency' number, for instance, so many man hours or pounds to make each product. Comparisons of these ratios can be highly informative (or misleading if misunderstood).

Legal, Planning and Insurance Requirements

The legal requirements of the country in which various activities of the project are undertaken must be met. Whilst it is not normal to list the laws of a 'host' country, it is possible that important or unusual requirements with respect to a particular job should be highlighted. These legal requirements may cover any subject, such as international trade, boycotts, working hours, expatriate staff permits, exchange control regulations and taxes, etc. Constant vigilance has to be maintained in order not to commit breaches of the law.

The restraints that may be imposed on a project by the planning authorities may be onerous. These conditions may change the initial conception of a project considerably. It is essential that the correct specialist staff, similar in function to those in the legal field, guide the initial stages of the job through the planning complexities. Then the appropriate warning notices must be issued in the job procedure.

Insurance obligations may be similar to legal and planning requirements. As far as jobs are concerned, it is important that staff are warned of difficult areas and know how to deal with them.

Consultants

There are areas of business or expertise that are best undertaken by a specialist firm acting as a consultant. Activities in the legal, marketing, special sciences or engineering, research, economics, banking and many other fields may fall into those areas where it is best to hire someone else to provide expertise. Naturally if one is going to use consultants in one field frequently it may become economic to set up a department for that speciality in one's own firm.

The engagement of consultants must be undertaken very carefully, as must the writing of their contract, so that they provide only services which are really required, and so that the services and all results and back-up data including, perhaps calculations, may be terminated, obtained at an intermediate point in the exercise, if the exercise has to be stopped before the end.

Consultants may be hired to perform a specific task, or to provide a service as requested on an intermittent basis. When first hiring consultants the full scope of work for them may be unknown (the consultant may be largely responsible for determining it). Take care that a runaway situation does not develop; carefully monitor the expenses, products and schedules of the consultant. Similarly, the professional consultant will check the client is asking for the right products, using them properly and not wasting his time and money.

Construction Aspects

So far the project procedures have described how the project is going to be organised. At the end of the project a new service, organisation, factory or facility is going to emerge. This facility itself has to be organised (see facilities operation) but before that it has to be constructed. Construction may be defined as assembling various components together to create a whole product. The activity of construction then requires definition and guidance. All sections of the procedure contribute towards construction, but more precise instructions are required for the assembly.

At this stage, before the project has developed far, it may be possible only to indicate the proposed or preferred method of assembly of components. Various services, contracts, items, many of which are not firm or finalised, require future development. It is only after the shape, scope, timing and quantity are definite that final construction can be detailed, but it is necessary at the beginning of the project to express a clear idea of the shape of the components so that during development all personnel are working on similar lines towards final interlocking assembly.

Many projects go through a phase in which there is a massive physical erection activity of mechanical components of a factory or facility. For this, decisions have to be made early in the job on how this phase will be managed, what sort of labour will be used, what the scope of subcontracts will be, the schedule for getting equipment to site and placing it in position or storing it, and how progress will be monitored for schedule, budget, quality and construction safety.

The Facilities Operation

This subject represents the ultimate estimate into the future, and, like any document describing future work (especially project procedures), will need revision whenever developments show that the way ahead is different from that which was estimated originally. The operation of facilities covers many facets of the actual running, renewal, maintenance and modification, training of personnel, records and spares keeping and the planning of future development, budgets and profitability.

After planning the services or equipment for the project, the documents covering the facility operation must be prepared. During the planning and specification stages of the project the operability of the facility is always a major factor to be considered. Detailed consideration of the facility operation may cause

modifications to be made to the original planning, but these must be minimised.

During the initial planning stage of the project, it may be necessary to mount a major study or investigation of financing, marketing or other activities that will be a continuous ongoing activity throughout the future life of the operating facility. Obviously it is pointless to execute a major project setting up a facility if one of the key normal activities of the facility is uneconomic. Whilst the construction project will have been set up only after pilot economic studies, these may well be carried further as part of the design or specification stage. Presumably the secondary studies will confirm the initial results, but they may also yield important data to be built into the operating procedures.

Operating procedures, written for the normal day-to-day business of the facility, may contain subjects such as those already mentioned in this article. The minimum operating procedures for all companies are the requirements of the Companies Act and the Health and Safety at Work Act which call for nominated personnel in certain functions and the annual audit and accounts. The opposite extreme is the directives, instructions and laws which control the operations of large international corporations and governments. Between these two extremes every significant facility requires its own specific operating procedures covering items not already included in the parental organisation's procedures for management, finance, technical and personnel departments.

This is one way to do the exercise

1 What do I know about project procedures?

Imagine that I am in charge of building a pyramid. How would I go about assembling the procedures that will be required? What do I know about procedures?

- Procedures are needed to make all project staff work in the same manner and direction
- Procedures will inform all need-to-know personnel of the project details
- Procedures require a team, communications, team leader, computer planning, monthly reviews, deadlines, delegation, rules, to be specified

2 Why am I reading this report, what are my OBJECTIVES?

I want to know:

- Who writes procedures and how?
- How are the procedures used by the project team?
- Will I be able to organise other projects' activities in a manner comparable with these procedures?

3 Carry out an overview

I do not write anything for this step. I glance through the whole report quickly, noting keywords or highlights.

The title is 'Management Tools – Project Planning Procedures'. That looks as if it will satisfy some of my objectives. The introduction confirms this.

Keywords – paragraph titles are:

Objectives
Job scope

Feasibility
Responsibilities
Organisation
Finance
Schedule
Control
Construction
Operation

Some of these look interesting and should be followed up in step five.

4 Preview

I reject those parts of the article which do not add to my knowledge, or do not meet my objectives. I zig-zag through the report to do this. Therefore, I will cross out the following paragraphs:

The plan
The basis of feasibility
Division of responsibilities
Financing arrangements
Agreements
Legal, planning and insurance
Consultants

5 Inview

I read those paragraphs which remain after the rejections made in the Preview step. As I read paragraphs or sections during my Inview stage I may find that more of these can be rejected, thus completing the Preview process, and shortening the Inview stage. Other paragraphs which should be studied more carefully when reading for the second or third time can be made to stand out by underlining, or with a line in the margin or using a coloured highlighter pen. The pace is steady and rhythmic. It is comfortable, taking several words in one fixation. It is the cruising speed.

6 Review

What parts of the article supply answers to the objective requirements? I now have to make notes or a recall pattern. I have
decided to answer each objective one by one. For objective
number one, I shall answer with traditional linear notes.

Who writes, and how are the procedures written?

There is no clear answer to this objective, so further reading
elsewhere will be necessary. However, the first paragraph of the
introduction to the report indicates that the Project Manager is
responsible for getting the procedures written. The Responsible
Personnel and Organisation Chart sections deal with the fact that
writing the procedures can be assigned to a suitable person on the
team. The fourth to seventh paragraphs of Administrative
Arrangements and the Plan of Execution help some way towards
the objective.

How are the procedures used by the project team?

To answer this objective, look at Figure 5.1, which shows a recall
pattern:

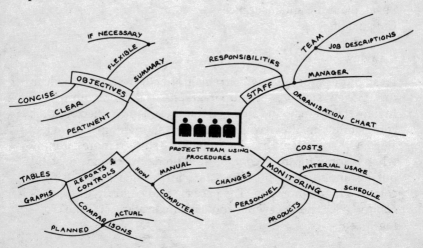

Figure 5.1 Recall pattern notes on project procedures

*Will I be able to organise other projects activities
in a manner comparable with these procedures?*

Yes! The report lists many of the factors which have to be considered in organising a project, and gives some guidelines on how they should be handled. Therefore it should be possible to assemble a list of factors for a specific project which will require procedures, and then to start drafting the procedures' contents.

6 Applying rapid reading to law reports

In this chapter . . .

> The systematic six-step method can be applied to material that is reputed to be precise and where 'every word counts'. The following example is taken from *The Law Society's Gazette*.
>
> As with the previous example report, we go through the same steps, but with different objectives in mind. Only one way is given to read the report. But there are many ways. The results depend primarily on the objectives set by the reader at the beginning and what information the document contains.
>
> In both examples we take the position of a layman who wishes to expand his knowledge of these subjects.

Time-sharing – the Club/Trustee System

by James Edmonds *

This is the third in a series of five articles on the subject of time-sharing. The most common structure for a time-sharing scheme is known as the club/trustee system and this article comments on that structure.

The most usual system utilised to set up a time-share scheme in the UK, Spain, Malta or Greece is the club/trustee system. The system is also used in Portugal and increasingly in other jurisdictions.

Under the club/trustee system the promoter becomes founder member of a club. The promoter then transfers the villas or

*Solicitor.

apartments to be time-shared to a trustee, to be held upon trust for the club members. The club rules divide the occupancy of each apartment or villa into 50 or 51 weekly periods, and provides that memberships are related to available occupancy periods, so that each member must be entitled to use one or more occupancy periods. The possible club membership is thus limited by the number of villas or apartments in trust and the number of weekly periods acquired by each member. The sole right of original appointment of new members is vested in the promoter, as founder member, but any member who derives title from the founder member can appoint a new member in his place, i.e. can sell or transfer his time-share.

The reason for the spread of the club/trustee system to civil law countries, unfamiliar with the Anglo-Saxon concept of trusts, is partly due to the UK market being the largest market for time-sharing, and partly due to the unique advantages of the concept over any alternative. The system is examined in more detail in the author's book *International Timesharing* (2nd edition).

Documentation

The initial documentation required to establish a club/trustee is the Club Constitution. The club is an unincorporated association whose members agree to be bound by a common set of rules and who together elect a committee to represent their interests. The rules of a time-share club must define the powers of the founder member (to appoint the original members) and restrict those powers so as to protect the interests of the membership generally. The rules must provide for the election of a committee, and its powers once elected, the allocation of running costs between members and many other matters of detail.

Secondly, a management agreement is needed. Usually the promoter is responsible for management at the outset, and incorporates a management company for this purpose. The management company is usually also made a founder member of the club, with powers for control of management to pass to an elected committee of members, once sufficient members have been appointed. The management agreement will define in more detail the allocation of expenses between members. The agreement will have to cater for different sized units and the introduction of more units into the scheme over a period. The agreement has to set out the responsibilities of the management company in some detail.

Thirdly, there is the trust deed which defines the responsibilities of the trustee to safeguard trust assets on behalf of club members, and to see that those assets are properly transferred, free of encumbrances, and that on-going responsibilities (e.g. payment of taxes, insurances, etc.) are discharged, so that the assets once transferred are not expropriated or destroyed without compensation. The role and responsibilities of the trustee go far beyond this, however, and will be examined below.

The final essential is the sales contract. This must identify the parties (surprisingly some do not!), the unit and the time periods. It should provide for payments to be made to an escrow agent (usually the trustee) not the promoter. The escrow provisions should effectively prevent the sale proceeds being handed over to the promoter, until the units have been vested in trust, free from encumbrances.

Consumer Protection

The two great advantages of the club/trustee system are consumer protection and flexibility. The keystone of the club/trustee system is of course the trustee. Provided that the trustee is independent, adequately capitalised and insured, and administratively equipped to deal with the time-share trust, a considerable degree of consumer protection can be achieved.

First, the promoter parts with his interest in the villas or apartments in exchange for the right to sell club memberships. Consequently, if the promoter becomes bankrupt or insolvent, a liquidator or receiver acquires only this right, not the ownership of the apartments or villas themselves. The existing members are therefore secure, and the property which they have a right to occupy will not be taken away from them.

Secondly, the trustee keeps, or should keep, details of every member and every unit in trust and every unit to be transferred into trust, so as to ensure that the membership is not sold more than once in the same week, and that the promoter does not obtain funds from sales in units not in trust. This is the fundamental reason why the deposit and purchase price should be paid to the trustee, and not to the promoter.

In several cases, the scheme has been set up properly at the outset, but the promoter is selling time-shares not only in units which have been bought and paid for, and transferred into trust, but also in units which have not been purchased or completed, or which are mortgaged. In the latter cases, the sale proceeds should be held by the trustee and not disbursed to the promoter until the units have been transferred into trust, free from encumbrances.

What sometimes happens, is that the promoter runs into what have been called cash-flow problems.

He then proceeds to open an account in his own name, reprints the contract to provide for payments direct to him, and banks and utilises the funds without telling the trustee. In the meantime the sales literature still includes references to the trustee so that purchasers are misled, believing that they are safeguarded, when that is not in fact the case. In the absence of legislation this puts the trustee in a very awkward position. Resignation by the trustee will only prejudice the interests of owners who are protected under the trust, since the owners who are protected may find it very difficult to persuade a reputable trustee to take on board what is bound then to be a messy situation.

Therefore, in a club trustee situation it is essential either to have the money paid to the trustee, or to obtain a certificate from the trustee that the particular unit being time-shared and week being sold is covered by the trust. A trustee which does not itself maintain ownership records may not always be able to establish with certainty who are the beneficiaries, i.e. who are protected by the trust.

Thirdly, the trustee should be responsible for administering the consumer protection aspects of the scheme, to see that moneys which are received by it are not disbursed until clear unencumbered title to the unit in question is transferred into trust, or that it is in possession of adequate guarantees that this will happen.

Where units are being constructed, and time-shares being sold in those units, the promoter often needs funds to pay for construction and marketing expenses. In such circumstances the trustee may be prepared to release from escrow funds covered by an independent guarantee from a bank, or from a substantial corporation, or secured on other assets. In some cases the building land can be transferred to the trustee at the outset, and the trustee can release up to a percentage of the value of the asset so transferred, on the basis that if the building works are not completed, the trustee may sell the assets and use the proceeds to reimburse the time-share purchasers.

Fourthly, there is the on-going responsibility of the trustee to safeguard trust assets. In many jurisdictions the properties themselves are subject to expropriation if taxes are not paid. So the trustee must ensure that the taxes are paid on time. A similar situation can arise in relation to community charges, e.g. *'communidades'* in Spain. The trustee must see to it that the properties are insured against fire and other perils. When the time-share owners re-sell, the trustee must record the change of beneficiary. Often where time-shares are pledged as security for a loan, the trustee will hold the certificate until the loan is paid off. Again, on re-sale, the trustee should be in a position to advise whether the maintenance charge has been paid, or whether the membership certificate has been forfeited for non-payment.

Finally, the independence, substance and administrative capability of the trustee is of paramount importance. Unfortunately some promoters are unable or unwilling to persuade a reputable trustee to act. This may be because of the record of the individual behind the scheme, or because the promoter cannot afford to have funds blocked in escrow, or that the promoter is unwilling to incur the cost or for a variety of other reasons. Also, many reputable trustees will not take on a trusteeship unless they are satisfied with the substance and qualification of the promoter. This has led to the formation by promoters of one-off trustee companies, often owned or controlled by the promoter and set up specially for the purpose. 'Off-the-shelf' trust companies can be formed in many jurisdictions without any capitalisation requirement beyond £2. The level of capitalisation of any trust company should be considered in the context of its professional indemnity policy (if any). Equally obviously, a trust company controlled, directly or through

nominees, by the scheme promoter, is hardly a proper guardian of the rights of those who purchase from that promoter. Again, some off-shore accountants or company formation agents are prepared to front for trust companies, without being able or willing to provide the high staffing requirement and degree of computerisation which may be thought desirable in the interests of effective management. Any practitioner advising in relation to a time-share project should make enquiries as to these matters.

Flexibility

The club trustee system is adaptable. In jurisdictions which do not recognise trusts, the assets can be transferred to a corporation incorporated in a jurisdiction which does recognise trusts, and the shares, as opposed to the property, vested in trust. If, as in Malta and certain parts of Greece, local law prevents acquisition of real property by foreign nationals, the rights can be secured by mortgage granted in favour of the trustee or its nominee, instead of a transfer of the title of the property itself.

Floating units, where the member has a right of occupation of a particular type of unit, as opposed to a specific unit, can also be created. The time-share right, once created, is easily transferable (most membership certificates have a form of transfer endorsed on the back of the certificate). The system lends itself to combination with escrow provisions, and the use of the certificate as security is easily achieved without cumbersome formality. Sales can be made in a chosen jurisdiction by using applications for memberships to be accepted in that jurisdiction, and combining this with management and promotional services agreements. This may have important tax and exchange control advantages. The transaction can be consummated quickly, and without burdensome registration formalities. The trustee can in fact operate the membership registry. The cost per sale is much less in a club/trustee system compared with a system which relies for its effectiveness on the registration of a freehold or leasehold interest in a public registry.

The formalities on involuntary devolution are less onerous (for example there is usually no need to obtain a grant of administration in a foreign jurisdiction). These advantages seem certain to secure an important role for the club/trustee system in the international development of time-sharing, particularly in view of the recent Hague Convention provision for overseas recognition of UK trusts. There is no doubt, however, that legislation is urgently needed to combat abuse of the system, to establish the minimum qualification of trustees, and mandatory requirements as to the provisions to be incorporated in the club/trustee documentation. The rules of the European Holiday Timeshare Association are a good indication as to what is required in this respect, and their regulations regarding trustees were derived from the Banking Act 1979 (licensed deposit takers) and the Public Trustee Rules 1911 (as amended).

1 Recall: What do I know about club time-sharing?

You buy a flat for, say, only four weeks of the year, for your own occupation. All the other weeks of the year are owned by other people, who occupy it on a similar basis. Usually this type of accommodation is abroad. Legally there are all sorts of problems. One must check on the soundness of the financial and legal basis of the development. Many people have lost all their money in time-share ventures. Then who is responsible for managing the flat and the whole complex? Check legal, administrative, financial and maintenance management.

2 Why am I reading this report? What are my objectives?

Having glanced through the article and spotted the subheading 'Consumer Protection':

- I want to be able to recognise an honest club system
- What differences are there between the law of England and other countries relating to this subject?

Remember that some objectives may not be answered by this document.

3 Overview

I note in the introduction (italics) that this is the third part of a five part series and not the last, so there is no final conclusion here today. The scheme is in operation in the UK and the Mediterranean countries. There are three subheadings: Documentation, Consumer Protection and Flexibility. Under 'Consumer Protection' paragraphs are clearly defined.

4 Preview The art of rejection

Keeping my objectives firmly in mind, I reject whatever does not respond to them. This includes the first two introductory paragraphs above the subheading 'Documentation'; under Flexibility, all I need to know is that the system is adaptable, so the rest seems irrelevant to my immediate concern.

5 Inview An in-depth reading of what I have not rejected

I am now reading steadily, with a rhythm. The columns are narrow, the vocabulary familiar, so I need one fixation per line. But I read each line. I want comprehension. If I feel I am going too fast, I slow down, but I do not regress.

Reading with a pencil – or highlighter – I am marking the keywords that answer my objectives.

The documentation is made up of four documents describing:

- An association held together by a set of rules
- A management agreement that defines the distribution of running costs between members

- A trust deed to safeguard assets of the members
- A sales contract identifying parties, time and unit involved.

A Club system has two essential advantages:

- Consumer protection
- Flexibility

It hinges on the trustee, an independent body. The trustee is responsible for the running costs of the units, so that if the promoter is bankrupt, dishonest or has ordinary cash-flow problems, the members keep their right to their properties. It means that monies are under the control of the trustee, records are kept by him/her and that monies are invested, or used appropriately. Anyone thinking of a time-share abroad should inquire about the total independence of the trustee, as promoters have been known to use 'off-the-shelf' companies to their own benefit, rather than that of their clients.

6 Review

Upon reviewing the objectives, the answers and the report, I notice that there is some information under the heading Flexibility that is interesting in its own right. So I will adopt a flexible approach and re-inview some of those paragraphs originally rejected. I am not much clearer about the differences between English and other countries' laws and will seek more information elsewhere.

Having got many of the answers to my objectives, here is a recall pattern.

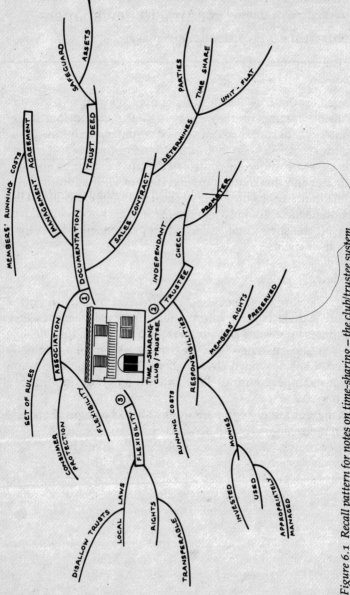

Figure 6.1 Recall pattern for notes on time-sharing – the club/trustee system

Crossing out a note lightly indicates that this note is a situation which is wrong

7 Applying rapid reading to newspapers, journals and meetings

In this chapter . . .

> Newspapers, journals and similar documents lend themselves well to rapid reading. The method is simplified as you need only a few of the six steps.
>
> Meetings can be modelled on a streamlined systematic approach to reading:
>
> ■ Objectives and Overview
> ■ Preview and Inview simultaneously
> ■ Review.
>
> Then we conclude by wishing you well on your journey of continuous discovery of knowledge.

Newspapers

Newspapers are divided into sections – home and international news, entertainments and arts reviews, sports, medical reports, business news, advertisements, and so on. If you buy the same newspaper every day, you become familiar with its presentation and style. Over the months, or years, you have practised 'Overviewing' your newspaper and you know where to find the type of information you are seeking. What changes every day, though, is the content.

As you move to a page that interests you, say international news, you should skim over it, noting headlines and selecting mentally those articles which you wish to read. When you are ready to read, a newspaper gives you an advantage over other printed material to practise conditioning: its narrow columns make it easy to have one fixation per line – perhaps even one per paragraph! You can go very fast.

A news article is constructed so that the most important information is contained in the opening paragraph; the rest is detail or reinforcement. Apply 'Previewing', paying attention to the beginning and exercising the art of rejection. Remember that a newspaper either summarises what happened yesterday, or anticipates on what may happen tomorrow. If you buy a newspaper or listen to the news every day, you have a lot of background information, and thus can dispense with most of the six systematic steps.

Let us consider an article from *The Times*.

Pöhl walks tightrope of German consensus

It is inconceivable in today's Britain that Robin Leigh-Pemberton would be reappointed Governor of the Bank of England had Mrs Thatcher lost the election. Indeed, his original appointment, before the 1983 election, proved so politically controversial that Labour would have pushed him out straight away had it won then. Luckily for the Germans, things are ordered differently in Bonn, where almost everyone is in favour of a monetary policy that will not permit rampant inflation. It was thus almost a formality that Karl Otto Pöhl gained a further eight-year term as President of the Bundesbank, though he was once as closely associated with the opposition Social Democrats, who appointed him, as Mr Leigh-Pemberton was with the Conservative Party.

Performance may also have something to do with it. The Governor is by no means certain of another term next year, since he has not always shown a safe pair of hands. Herr Pöhl, by contrast, has emerged as one of the two most influential central bankers in international discussion of exchange rate and monetary co-operation. Since the other, Paul Volcker, is on the way out, Herr Pöhl is likely to be called on for leadership.

He will not be giving an unequivocal message. The Bundesbank has recently used an exchange rate target for monetary policy almost as much as the Treasury and the Bank of England and has likewise exceeded its targets for monetary growth. There are two differences. West Germany still has negligible inflation, mainly thanks to the improving terms of trade – though this could change if dollar weakness persists into a period of rising commodity prices. And, as Herr Pöhl made clear yesterday, the Bundesbank feels guilty about exceeding monetary targets, while the British authorities prefer to pretend nothing is amiss.

The great strength of German monetary policy, however, is the overt restriction on its scope. Monetary targets are set to accommodate the expected trends in the economy without inflation (or deflation). They are not used, as in Britain, or especially the United States, as a principal lever on the economy. The reluctance of the Germans to engage in a positive policy of cutting interest rates to stimulate their sluggish economy is, for this reason, often misinterpreted as excessive caution.

The continuing message from Herr Pöhl will surely be that less weight be placed on monetary management as a policy tool.

Fiscal policy is to stimulate or rein back demand and direct action should be used to help stabilize exchange rates within that framework. In that context, Herr Pöhl has proved a constant and persuasive lobbyist for sterling to be fixed to the EMS.

German monetary policy has worked partly because history has produced a consensus fearful of inflation but also because the independent central bank has not been obliged, like Mr Volcker, to bear too much of the burden of economic management. This is an important message for Herr Pöhl to evangelize, not least at home where his opposite number, the finance minister Gerhard Stoltenburg, despite the supposedly close working relationship between the two, has not been as adventurous as he might have been in cutting taxes, liberalizing the economy and boosting domestic demand to replace exports.

This article illustrates the nature of newspaper material. The opening paragraph compares the heads of Britain's and Germany's central banks – bringing the reader quickly into perspective; it sets the scene.

The second, third and fourth paragraphs refresh the reader's mind about inflation in Germany and the German position on monetary policy. It does not impart any new knowledge.

The penultimate and last paragraphs open up new ideas:

1 The desire of the Germans to have sterling within the EMS
2 The possible strategies Herr Pöhl and the Finance Minister can use in order to boost the German economy.

If you usually keep an eye on European economic affairs, you need to read the first, penultimate and last paragraphs only.

Journals

The main trouble with journals is the frequency with which they appear in your in-tray. Journals are aimed at a professional body but, within this, include a variety of subjects aimed at reaching all their readership with at least one article per issue. Overview the whole journal by looking at the pages of contents. Note the article or articles you may want to read. Preview by turning to the appropriate pages and then locate and read the synopsis and conclusion. If there is none, read the opening and concluding paragraphs. If you decide you need more information, read the rest, using the conditioning approach, looking for key ideas and using a guide.

If you own the copy of the journal and are not interested in the advertising, tear it apart so that you save only the article(s) you need.

Let us take as an example an article from *The Economist*.

Banking Brief

Deutsche makes its mark

While Deutsche Bank expands abroad, at home its power as a do-everything banker, adviser and part-owner of huge chunks of West German industry is under attack

It is as hard to keep Deutsche Bank down as to discover its true wealth. The bank was founded in Berlin in 1870 to finance Germany's fast-expanding industry and foreign trade. It lost most of its assets after the second world war and was split up by the occupying powers. The bank was re-united in Frankfurt in 1957 and was immediately busy building a domestic branch network to cope with a surge in business during the West German 'economic miracle' years. It was slower at rebuilding its foreign presence because it was nervous that it would meet resistance, even hostility, abroad as a consequence of lingering hatred against the Germans after the war.

When the bank did venture outside West Germany, it usually did so in collaboration with non-German banks. Other big West German banks were as cautious, but Deutsche has easily outstripped them. It has coasted through the past few years with firm profits and regular dividends.

Probably the best guide to the true earnings of Deutsche Bank would be its overall group operating profit. But, like other German banks, Deutsche will officially disclose only its 'partial' operating profit – which excludes the often-hefty profits from own-account trading in securities and foreign exchange. The bank's net profit is, more or less, what it chooses to put on the final line of its accounts.

This is allowed under German accounting rules, although it makes for an analyst's nightmare. However, it can be reliably reckoned that the overall group operating profit of the bank exceeded DM5 billion ($2.3 billion) in 1986. That is more than the combined estimated operating profits of Dresdner Bank and Commerzbank, the other two big West German private-sector banks.

Total loan-loss reserves are not disclosed either. But Deutsche has stashed away enough money to cover roughly two-thirds of its loans to developing countries. Its consolidated loan-loss reserves (for domestic and foreign risks) probably total more than DM10 billion. This is a thick cushion against future difficulties and it is the envy of many big American banks.

Even the figures which are made public still underline Deutsche Bank's premier position in Germany. From the two crystal towers of its Frankfurt headquarters (known as 'credit' and 'debit'), Deutsche serves 6.6m customers with 50,000 employees at 1,410 branches, 65 of them outside West Germany. The bank's total assets in 1986 were DM257.2 billion (compared with the DM196.8 billion of the Dresdner Bank) and it had a hoard of cheap funds – DM24.5 billion on deposit from thrifty German savers.

Deutsche also holds stakes, direct and indirect, in some of Germany's biggest companies (see table), and members of its management board sit on the supervisory boards of dozens of other companies. What are these holdings worth? The bank gives the 1986 book value of its 'subsidiaries, affiliated companies and trade investments' as DM6.5 billion – but the market value of its most prized stake (just over 28% of Daimler-Benz, West Germany's prosperous and diversifying carmaker) is alone worth roughly double that.

The *Depotstimmrecht* also adds to the power of Deutsche. This is a system through which West German banks vote at company annual meetings on behalf of customers who, in the German tradition of letting the bank handle just about every detail of their financial affairs, deposit their shares with them. Yet, despite being the biggest fish in its prosperous domestic pond, Deutsche still ranks only 14th internationally in terms of its assets (see chart).

Deutsche Bank has tried to squeeze every drop of business out of its home market by, for instance, combining a savings plan with insurance and recently with a push into building finance. But West Germany's capital market has long been small and timid, although it is now getting bigger and livelier. The retail banking business is also overcrowded (with 4,700 banks operating nearly 40,000 branches). Too many banks are competing to serve a German population which is shrinking because of the country's extraordinarily low birthrate. Really big growth has to come from abroad.

Adventures abroad

Deutsche Bank has expanded its foreign operations, both in commercial banking and in investment banking (i.e. securities trading and portfolio management). It plans to expand further in:

■ **Commercial banking.** In December 1986, Deutsche Bank made its biggest foreign investment, so far. It bought the Banca d'America e d'Italia from the troubled Bank of America for about $600m. This gave Deutsche access to the Italian retail banking market, through one of Italy's most profitable banks, with 3,000 employees and about 100 branches. More expansion in Europe is planned. Deutsche reckons that a single, unified EEC financial market will come along, although it might be later than the Community's official target date of 1992.

Where will Deutsche look to expand in Europe next? Its rule of thumb is to seek majority stakes, but not to attack a market in a country already dominated by a small group of about four domestic banks. That could exclude countries like Belgium, Britain and France. Spain, though, would be a likely candidate.

Further afield, Deutsche also last year acquired full control of the former European Asian Bank (Eurasbank), which it renamed Deutsche Bank (Asia). That provided 20 more branches in 12 Asian countries, in addition to Deutsche's existing network in the region. Deutsche had founded the Eurasbank in 1972 with members of a consortium, European Banks International. It bought out its partners, one by one.

■ **Investment banking.** Here, Deutsche's efforts are directed at the world's leading capital markets: Tokyo, New York and

London. Its Tokyo capital-markets branch began operations last year, trading in Japanese and foreign securities. Technically, the Tokyo branch is an offshoot of Deutsche's Hongkong capital-markets operation and only half-owned, to comply with Japanese rules. It is, however, the core of Deutsche Bank's Asian network, which extends to Singapore and Australia. To raise its profile in the region, Deutsche Bank will have its shares listed on the Tokyo stock exchange in November.

The New York investment-banking arm, Deutsche Bank Capital Corporation, began under another name with Swiss partners, which were later bought out. Deutsche is the biggest market-maker in German shares in America (an under-developed market, admittedly, because opaque German accounting worries American investors) and scoops up American pension-fund money for international investment. It has more than $1 billion under management. More corporate finance, including mergers and acquisitions business, will be the next steps. Deutsche also wants to enter the American Treasury bond market, either by buying into an existing primary dealership or by building up its own capacity (more likely).

In London, it set up Deutsche Bank Capital Markets in 1985 and moved its non-D-mark Eurobond business there from Frankfurt. That shocked many people in the Frankfurt financial establishment and prodded Germany's central bank, the Bundesbank, into giving its capital market a facelift. For several years, Deutsche has figured among the top lead-managers of Eurobond and note issues, pipped only by the London-based joint venture, Credit Suisse First Boston and, lately, by the top Japanese securities firms.

Despite that, Deutsche is meek about its investment-banking skills, especially in mergers and acquisitions business. So it also bought a 4.9% stake in Morgan Grenfell, an accident-prone British merchant bank, saying it wanted to learn more about international investment banking. Some people scoffed at that explanation, but it was true.

Less ostentatious are Deutsche's Geneva and Zurich operations, catering for clients who want a bank combining Swiss discretion with Deutsche's links in international centres. The published figures do not tell much, but Deutsche Bank's Swiss operation is getting a steady flow of new customers – maybe one reason that Swiss banks are countering by setting up shop in Frankfurt.

Deutsche Bank's expansion has not always been smooth. For example, before Deutsche gained full control of the Eurasbank it had to provide – with the help of its

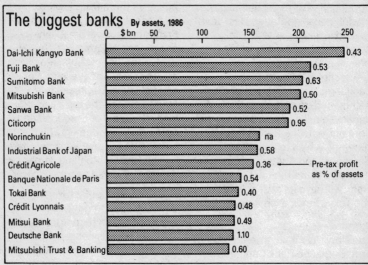

The biggest banks   By assets, 1986

Bank	Pre-tax profit as % of assets
Dai-Ichi Kangyo Bank	0.43
Fuji Bank	0.53
Sumitomo Bank	0.63
Mitsubishi Bank	0.50
Sanwa Bank	0.52
Citicorp	0.95
Norinchukin	na
Industrial Bank of Japan	0.58
Crédit Agricole	0.36
Banque Nationale de Paris	0.54
Tokai Bank	0.40
Crédit Lyonnais	0.48
Mitsui Bank	0.49
Deutsche Bank	1.10
Mitsubishi Trust & Banking	0.60

Source: The Banker

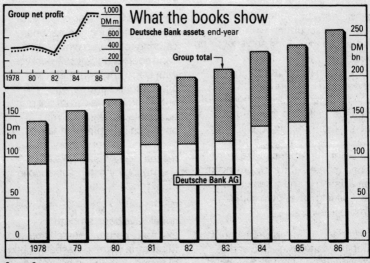

Group net profit

What the books show

Deutsche Bank assets end-year

Group total

Deutsche Bank AG

Source: Company reports

other shareholders – for heavy losses from bad loans, particularly industrial and property loans in Taiwan, Hongkong and Singapore. The London capital-markets operation also had teething problems. There were internal squabbles and some of Deutsche's Euromarket stars stumped off in a huff. This was a sign of a deeper problem facing the bank.

Until a few years ago, investment banking at Deutsche did not have the weight and prestige of the commercial-banking side. Swaps, floating-rate notes and the other paraphernalia of the international capital markets were treated with suspicion – certainly by the Bundesbank, which banned them in domestic German markets until 1985.

Much has changed. Investment-banking activities are reckoned to have contributed about 40% of overall profits last year, and in some months more than half. But a long debate within the bank, over several years, about whether to set up shop in London and if so when, alienated some of the bank's more impatient spirits. Its critics reckoned this showed a lack of flair and an inability to react quickly, blaming it on the bank's collegiate management style.

First among equals

Like some other West German banks, Deutsche's management board does not have a chief executive. It follows a principle of collective leadership, in which one member of the board may be appointed as its 'spokesman'. Deutsche Bank takes equality further. It has two managing-board spokesmen: Mr Friedrich Wilhelm Christians and Mr Alfred Herrhausen. They are not, however, even identified as such in the bank's annual report. This simply lists all 10 full board members alphabetically.

Each member of the board (average salary, DM1.4m) also has responsibility for an area of domestic business in addition to any international role. This is supposed to keep their feet on the ground. Although boardroom discussions are reputedly forthright, decisions must be taken unanimously or not at all. It was not always like that.

When the bank was built up after the second world war, there was just one figure visibly at the helm: Mr Hermann Josef Abs, a man of implacable will and the mild appearance of a country squire, who stepped down in 1967. At the age of 85, he remains honorary president. Two spokesmen were chosen to succeed Mr Abs and (apart from a short period) two board members have continued to be appointed to the job. But will the arrangement last?

Mr Christians, aged 65, retires next year. He is an equity-market expert and has been co-spokesman since 1976. The managing board will decide who among them will replace him. There are a number of hopefuls for the job. The front runners are: Mr Werner Blessing, aged 56, whose responsibilities include Latin America; Mr Ulrich Weiss, aged 51, responsible for the bank's internal organisation and its data-processing; and Mr Herbert Zapp, aged 59, who is in charge of company customers, venture capital – and the modern-art displays which adorn the bank's headquarters. A dark horse is Mr Hilmar Kopper, aged 52, responsible for Europe, including Comecon. He pulled off the Banca d'America e d'Italia purchase (after first deciding against it).

The board could, however, decide to let 57-year-old Mr Herrhausen continue on his own. He joined the bank from the VEW energy company in 1970 and became co-spokesman in 1985. Mr Herrhausen has many contacts in West Germany, including a good line to Mr Helmut Kohl, the West German chancellor. He might need them. Although some people, inside and outside the bank, reckon Deutsche could benefit again with one man at the top, he would draw more fire from the bank's critics.

Mr Herrhausen is also chairman of the supervisory board of Daimler-Benz, West Germany's biggest company in terms of sales, which has diversified away from

being a car and lorry manufacturer into electronics and aerospace. Having the top job at Deutsche, as well as the post at Daimler-Benz, would mean a concentration of power in the hands of one man not seen since the days of Mr Abs (who had posts on more than 20 supervisory boards). It would bring more pressure – not only from West Germany's political left – for new laws to curb what is sometimes called 'the power of the banks', or more particularly, the power of Deutsche Bank.

Deutsche has already been chided for the way it has used its influence at Daimler-Benz. On July 13th, Mr Werner Breitschwerdt, the chief executive of Daimler-Benz, ended months of speculation about his future when it was announced that he would prematurely give up his job. It was thanks to Deutsche's casting vote in 1983 that Mr Breitschwerdt got his job, despite opposition from representatives of the labour force on the supervisory board. After Mr Herrhausen became Deutsche's co-spokesman in 1985, the bank appeared to change its mind about Mr Breitschwerdt.

Friction like that fuels the debate in West Germany over the influence of its banks. Some people argue that Deutsche Bank has plenty of international banking challenges to face without continuing to play nanny to German industry. If the bank were to be bold, it could deflate its critics by reducing its stake in Daimler-Benz, giving up the chairmanship of its supervisory board, and a few others elsewhere. Some of Deutsche's board members even argue that their supervisory-board work is a burden they could well do without.

Deutsche Bank's main company holdings *

Company	Business
Direct holdings	
Bergmann-Elektricitäts-Werke	Holding company
Daimler-Benz	Vehicles, electricals & aerospace
Deutsche Dampfschifffahrts-Gesellschaft 'Hansa'	Shipping
Hapag-Lloyd	Shipping and tourism
Philipp Holzmann	Building
Karstadt	Retailing
Süddeutsche Zucker-AG	Sugar
Indirect holdings	
Metallgesellschaft	Metal processing and engineering
Horten	Retailing
VEW (Westphalia)	Electricity utility
Hutschenreuther	Porcelain manufacturer
Didier-Werke	Engineering

Source: Company report   *Of at least 25% in 1986

Applying rapid reading to this article:

1 What do I know?

Not very much about the Deutsche Bank *per se*. I only know that German banks are powerful and that the average German prefers to settle his bills using cash or cheques. Credit cards have not caught on in Germany.

2 Set objectives

To gain an overall knowledge of Deutsche Bank, particularly with respect to its influence abroad.

3 Overview

The article describes;

- history of the bank
- approximate operating profits, reserves and assets. Limit to growth in W. Germany
- past and future expansion abroad – commercial
  – investment
- structure of management board
- relationship with Daimler Benz

4 Preview and inview (Combine them for this example)

I skim through the past history. I read more slowly the passage dealing with links with industry (7th, 8th and 9th paragraphs). I read with care – using a cruising speed – the whole section headed 'Adventures Abroad'. I skim through 'First Among Equals' as this seems more directed to internal history and politics. I didn't know that the Japanese and French were so prominent in this field. Better check if the Japanese definition of a bank is the same as that in the west.

5 Review

Make a recall pattern for notes. (See figure 7.1).

Meetings

You can handle a meeting the same way you handle a book. All we need to do is change the wording.

Normally, when you are asked to a meeting you know why, you know the broad lines. That is what an agenda is for – the objectives. If you do not have agendas, maybe your office should review the way it organises meetings. In this case, you can jot down, using a recall pattern, the possible issues to be discussed. This is your **overview**.

As you listen to the information, you use **previewing** and **inviewing** simultaneously. The previewing allows you to con-

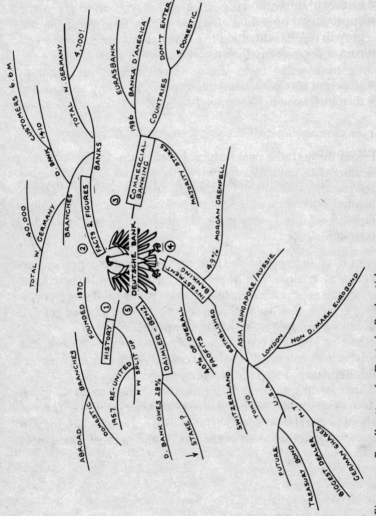

Figure 7.1 Recall pattern for Deutsche Bank article

nect ideas together quickly, and inviewing occurs when you question the speaker on a point of particular interest. To keep your concentration and for future reference, you make notes. Using recall patterns makes it easier, as you were given the structure with the agenda. Also new information, questions and corrections can be added easily to the pattern notes, where you have more accessibility than to notes made in a linear style.

After the meeting, review the notes to reinforce your long-term memory and fill your knowledge gaps. Pick up any outstanding points which need to be followed up later.

Conclusion

The key objectives this book set out to achieve were to give you:

- confidence
- technique
- flexibility

If you have improved your reading speed and comprehension you can maintain and improve them further. Regular practice is the key to keeping and improving a newly acquired skill. As you become more familiar with the technique, you can, of course, tailor it to your own style and requirements.

Some of you will have found each step easy to absorb and apply, others will not. In the latter case, it is a matter of perseverance. Repeat each step until it becomes second nature.

Rapid reading expands your capacity to concentrate, sharpens your memory and permits you to widen your interests. There is no limit to your latent talents. This book is only the beginning. Go out and tackle other areas of knowledge and interest. Good luck!

References and bibliography

References and books related to rapid reading that I found helpful.

The Brain

'A review of right hemisphere linguistic capabilities', A. SEARLEMAN, *Psychological Bulletin*, 1977, Vol. 84 No. 3

The Brain Book, PETER RUSSELL, Routledge & Kegan Paul, London

Left Handed: Right Handed, MARK BROWN, David and Charles, Newton Abbot

The Universe Within, MORTON HUNT, Corgi, London

The Working Brain, A. R. LURIA, Penguin, London

Programs of the Brain, J. Z. YOUNG, Oxford University Press, Oxford

Build Your Brain Power, ARTHUR WINTER, MD, and RUTH WINTER, St Martin's Press (USA)

The Mind, ANTHONY SMITH, Viking, London

Reading

Rapid Reading Made Simple, GORDON WAINWRIGHT, W. H. Allen, London

Use Your Head, TONY BUZAN, Ariel Publications, London

Speed Reading, TONY BUZAN, David and Charles, Newton Abbot

Speedreading, FINK, TATE & ROSE, John Wiley, Chichester

'How to read faster and better', F. J. AGARDY/*Evelyn Wood* in *Reading Dynamics*, Simon & Schuster (USA)

Dyslexia

This Book Doesn't Make Sense, JEAN AUGUR

Overcoming Dyslexia, B. HORNSBY, Martin Dunitz, London

Dyslexia: What Parents Ought To Know, ALAN MCAUSLAN, Penguin, London

THE BRITISH DYSLEXIA ASSOCIATION,
Church Lane,
Peppard,
Oxfordshire RG9 5JN
This has many local associations

THE DYSLEXIA INSTITUTE,
133 Gresham Road,
Staines,
Middlesex TW18 2AJ

Eyes

Better Sight Without Glasses, W. H. BATES, Thorsons, Wellingborough
The Art of Seeing, A. HUXLEY, Granada, London

Management

Understanding Organisations, CHARLES B. HANDY, Penguin, London
The Aquarian Conspiracy, MARILYN FERGUSON, Paladin Granada, London
Future Shock, ALVIN TOFLER, Bodley Head, London
'Management Tools – Project Planning Procedures', K. REDWAY,
    Industrial Management & Data Systems, MCB University Press, Sept. 85

Miscellaneous

The Europeans, LUIGI BARZINI, Weidenfeld & Nicolson, London
The Mind of a Mnemonist, A. R. LURIA, Penguin, London
Effective Speaking, CRISTINA STUART, Pan, London
I Keep Six Honest Serving-Men, R. KIPLING
Oxford English Dictionary
'Time-sharing – the Club/Trustee System', JAMES EDMONDS, *The Law
    Society's Gazette*, 7 Jan. 87
'Pöhl walks tightrope of German consensus', *The Times*, 25 June 87
'Deutsche Makes its Mark', Banking Brief from *The Economist*,
    25 July 1987

Index

Make the Most of Your Mind £3.99

Tony Buzan

A straightforward and sensible handbook explaining clearly how your brain works and how you can use it more effectively.

This practical short course will enable you to tap more of your brain's vast potential and will be valuable for anyone keen to learn, read, memorize and think more efficiently.

This up-dated and expanded edition includes a new chapter highlighting the benefits of group study and a series of full colour diagrams that will help you make the most of any learning situation.

All these books are available at your local bookshop or newsagent, or can be ordered direct from the publisher. Indicate the number of copies required and fill in the form below.

Send to: **CS Department, Pan Books Ltd., P.O. Box 40, Basingstoke, Hants.   RG21 2YT.**

or phone: 0256 469551 (Ansaphone), quoting title, author and Credit Card number.

Please enclose a remittance* to the value of the cover price plus: 60p for the first book plus 30p per copy for each additional book ordered to a maximum charge of £2.40 to cover postage and packing.

*Payment may be made in sterling by UK personal cheque, postal order, sterling draft or international money order, made payable to Pan Books Ltd.

Alternatively by Barclaycard/Access:

Card No.

Signature:

Applicable only in the UK and Republic of Ireland.

While every effort is made to keep prices low, it is sometimes necessary to increase prices at short notice. Pan Books reserve the right to show on covers and charge new retail prices which may differ from those advertised in the text or elsewhere.

NAME AND ADDRESS IN BLOCK LETTERS PLEASE:

....

Name————————————————————————

Address—————————————————————————